The Frozen Toe Guide to Real Alaskan Livin'

Learn How to Survive Moose Attacks, Endless Winters & Life Without Indoor Plumbing

BROOKELYN BELLINGER

Printed in the United States of America
Published by Sasquatch Books
Distributed by Publishers Group West
15 14 13 12 11 10 09 08 07   9 8 7 6 5 4 3 2 1

Cover photograph: © Gerry Johansson (UK)/Photonica/Getty Images
Cover design by Judith Stagnitto Abbate/Abbate Design
Interior design and composition: Rosebud Eustace

ISBN: 1-57061-484-9

Library of Congress Cataloging-in-Publication Data is available.

Sasquatch Books
119 South Main Street, Suite 400
Seattle, WA 98104
(206) 467-4300
www.sasquatchbooks.com
custserv@sasquatchbooks.com

Contents

Acknowledgments

This book is dedicated to _____ (your name here), the fine consumer who got lucky and found this book in stock at _____ (location), or was given this book as a gift, in which case I'm _____ (adjective) for you. This small act of kindness has helped me to put _____ (object) on the table for my family, dogs, future chickens, and perhaps a reindeer or two. Thank you! I hope you find this to be a _____ (adjective) guide that may inspire you to try _____ (action) or _____ (action). It may even cajole you into joining us up here in Alaska permanently or determine your _____ (adjective) departure.

For now, _____ (verb) up and yell _____ (exclamation) because you have this book in your hands.

Thanks again. I mean it.

_____

(Forge author's name here for added resale value.)

Introduction

I figured most people would skip over the introduction—I usually do. But here you are, so let me think of something quick: OK, what you have here in your hands is something pretty special. It's filled with all the wacky and wonderful realities that define Alaskan living. And this stuff is raw—there's no sugar coating here. There are no fluffy bears or listings for cheap tourist T-shirts. Here you will find outhouse races and giant vegetables, extreme racing athletes and moose attack survivors. Here is advice on how to endure Alaska's brutal winters without succumbing to constant inebriation, along with ideas for finding sleep under the midnight sun and how to develop a fashionable coffee addiction. You will also find uniquely Alaskan recipes, like homemade cinnamon rose hip tea or cranberry liqueur, and instructions for how to eat sea urchin roe on crackers. And, in case you were wondering, you will learn how to dress like an Alaskan. (This is not always pretty.) This book is really a smorgasbord of equal parts entertainment and information with just a bit of crap mixed in.

As you read along, you may notice that I mention the wearing of chicken suits quite often. These are just the unrealized dreams of this author coming true through the pages of this book and should not be seen as a reflection of Alaskans as a whole.

Since my name is listed as author, I would like to take this opportunity to thank you for buying this book, and in the same breath, would now like to release myself from any liability that may arise from your actually heeding any advice herein. Just have a good time and be safe out there. (Always carry a gun.)

1

Dreaming of Alaska:
Go Your Own Way

Every Alaskan has their own story about how they got here and how they survived their first few months. My story involves a bad haircut, a duct-taped tent, and an unfortunate moose encounter. Despite those setbacks, I'm still here, and I have some advice for those thinking of joining all the other crazy people who have already made their journey north.

HELLO ALASKA, HOW DO YA LIKE MY HAIR?

It was inevitable that I would end up in Alaska someday. Growing up in Michigan, I had always been an outdoor girl. I liked to hang out in the woods, liked to climb trees and stalk deer—sometimes shoot them. In other words, I had a deep appreciation for the natural world. You could also say I wasn't very cool. I was a tomboy. I'll never forget a comment I got one day in high school gym class. This was the '80s—when "big hair" and feathered bangs were in. Now, imagine a short version of a bob, cut just above the ears, and that's what I had. This boy said to me, "You look like a penis head." I have to admit, it wasn't the look I was going for.

Adversity can only make a person stronger. Even with my penis-head haircut, I managed to land a boyfriend. He lived on a farm and we made deer blinds, shot guns, trapped muskrats, and shoveled cow manure together. It was a glorious time. But good times can't last, and we broke up. In retaliation, I grew out my hair in a Farrah Fawcett hair–worship sort of way and made my way West, taking on various outdoor jobs. I yearned for Alaska—a place where all kinds of oddballs fit in. A place where hunters, greenies, hippies, and conservatives alike all lived for the same reasons: that spirited Alaskan independence, wide-open spaces, the oil check, and a plethora of espresso stands. So with $200 to spare, I grabbed my backpack and bought a ticket to the Last Frontier. I arrived in Anchorage after a long flight, slept in the airport till dawn (3:00 a.m.), and caught a shuttle to Homer. It was raining when I got there and almost dark. When I asked about camping, the shuttle driver mentioned something about a bed and breakfast that had a bunkroom, and for $15 I could sleep there for the night—breakfast included. I had hit the cheap jackpot (never again to be experienced in Alaska).

SIX REASONS TO MOVE TO ALASKA

1 The oil check

2 Flannel shirts are cool

3 Bon Jovi doesn't tour here

4 No state taxes

5 The northern lights

6 You don't need an excuse to vacation in Hawaii

Within a week and a half I had two jobs and was collecting my first paycheck. I worked out a deal with the owner of the B&B: I would help out with the cooking and cleaning, and in exchange she would let me live on the property in my tent. I also got a job at a fishing/tackle shop selling all but rockets and mortars for killing fish.

Life was good—fishing, work, and socializing took most of my time. Once in a while I'd lie on my back with my head sticking out of the tent door and just stare at the sky, thinking just how lucky I was. One night, as I drifted with my thoughts, the ground began to shake, and in a sudden rush of commotion a large moose ran by, missing my face by an inch. I sat up quick—my scalp burning. When I caught my breath, I looked around and found a huge wad of hair lying on the grass in front of my tent. The moose had stepped on my perfect feathered hair and pulled out several large chunks. Imagine a haircut David Letterman might give after three drinks, and there's your visual. I had no choice but to revert to short hair. But not to worry—men in Alaska aren't that picky. All I had to say was, "Do you know any good fishing spots?" and I had myself a boyfriend—and a man with a shotgun for future "defense of life" situations.

Besides the B&B guest that got drunk and sang John Denver tunes all night and the unfortunate moose "event," my summer was absolutely perfect. You too can find this kind of satisfaction up here in Alaska. There are untold adventures waiting—and we'll welcome you no matter what your haircut.

A Newcomer's Guide to Alaska

The following glossary of terms used by Alaskans on a daily basis is offered as a service to newcomers confused by our regional colloquialisms, and is provided by David A. James, Regional Colloquialisms Specialist from Fairbanks.

Cheechako:

Derogatory term used to describe anyone who arrived in Alaska more than twenty seconds after the person using the term. A cheechako is an ignoramus who hasn't lived here long enough to clearly understand how things work. Those of you planning on moving to Alaska should, if coming by land, pass as many vehicles as possible on the Al-Can. If coming by air, claw your way to the front of the cabin upon landing in order to be the first to deplane. Anyone behind you upon arrival will, by definition, be your inferior.

Lower 48:

Analogous to Purgatory. Refers to the forty-eight contiguous states that are notable for their heavy traffic, high crime rates, and concentrations of relatives most Alaskans quite deliberately left behind. Also the location of good shopping, genuine cultural opportunities, and plenty of gullible folks who will believe absolutely anything they are told about Alaska. Note: There is also a Lower 50th, better known as Hawaii, which Alaskans look upon with a mixture of envy and longing, particularly in January.

Indoor plumbing:

Technological advance that greatly enhanced the daily lives of citizens of the Roman Empire. Still a novelty for many Alaskans.

Outside:

When capitalized, this term is similar to, but not synonymous with, "Lower 48." "Outside" is anywhere beyond the borders of Alaska and is to be feared and avoided. When lowercase, "outside" refers to the outdoors, a place where any real Alaskan has kept out of ever since getting indoor plumbing and that lovely satellite dish.

PFD (Permanent Fund Dividend):

Annual check the state provides to every legal resident, regardless of age. Also the primary reason most people live here. The true sign of Alaska manhood is to sire at least fifteen children and confiscate their PFDs in October so that a down payment can be made on a decent snowmachine.

Jimmy Carter:

Peanut farmer and thirty-ninth president of the United States who set aside large swaths of pristine Alaska wilderness for future generations to enjoy and became subsequently reviled statewide as the cause of every problem in Alaska. Did you put your SUV in the ditch? Did you lose your mining job because you showed up drunk? Are you in jail? Relax, it's Jimmy Carter's fault, not yours.

Transfer station:

Location of dumpsters from which many Alaskans obtain a decent living. Social status in Fairbanks circles is always enhanced when one makes a good find at the transfer station. It's not dumpster diving, it's wealth acquisition.

Salcha:

Small, widely dispersed community along the Richardson Highway to the southeast of Fairbanks. Where people move when they decide North Pole is just a tad too liberal for their tastes.

Wedding shower:

Prenuptial bathing ritual undertaken by residents of Goldstream Valley who are otherwise not noted for exemplary personal hygiene. These showers are generally taken in large groups in order to save shower stall fees at the Laundromat.

AIP (Alaskan Independence Party):

Kind of like the NRA on methamphetamines. Avoid these people at all costs.

Bush Democrat:

Not, as it seems, a Democrat who for some strange, inexplicable reason voted for George W. Bush. Rather, this refers to residents of rural Alaska—known as "the Bush"—who for some strange, inexplicable reason vote Democrat. Either way, it doesn't make much sense.

Gas line:

Long-hoped-for pipeline that will convert hot air emanated by politicians into a saleable (and renewable) resource.

Uncle Ted:

U.S. senator Ted Stevens, hero of all Alaska. Noted magician who makes money appear from nowhere and who spreads it across the state. The biggest fear of any Alaskan is the thought of Uncle Ted's magic wearing off, causing Alaska's economy to collapse.

Sourdough:

Name for someone who has lived in Alaska long enough to clearly understand how things work up here. "Sour" refers to the expression on his face as well as the scent escaping from his bunny boots. "Dough" is what he lacks.

Reprinted with the permission of David A. James from an article first published in the Fairbanks Daily News-Miner.

DRIVE TO ALASKA

The most spectacular road trip of your life will be the one that leads to Alaska. There is no finer way of seeing the country, no matter where you're coming from. You will cross the most scenic and rugged country that North America has to offer. And don't worry, you don't need a brand-new car to make the journey. A reliable older model will do just fine. Just prepare for the unexpected. Take an extra tire or two, a tire repair kit, a bicycle pump, an extra 5 gallons of gas, maybe some belts and hoses, a gallon of water, extra oil, flares, etc. For the most part, folks will stop and help if you do break down—especially if it's a long way to the next town. And contrary to popular belief, the roads are mainly paved and in decent shape. There will inevitably be road construction—so be prepared to deal with it. Summer is the only time that workers can repair road damage, so just be patient, and remember where that road is taking you.

It doesn't have to cost a lot to drive to Alaska. In fact, it can be one of the cheapest and most exciting ways to get yourself north. We never sleep in motels. It is a rare snowstorm in early or late summer that will force us to give up some of our hard-earned cash for a comfy bed, but it's usually worth it at least once in the journey. Otherwise, we sleep hunched in our seats or find a place to pitch our tent. The former can leave you with just enough sleep to get back on the road at a decent hour with a crook in your neck, while the latter can consume an extra hour or two of set-up and take-down but can produce a decent night's sleep. Clearly a dilemma. There are lots of pull-offs and waysides to catch a wink during the day too, if needed. If you are fortunate enough to own a pickup camper or an RV, count yourself among the blessed. Showers are easy enough to find along the way too.

Food can be brought along in coolers. Supplies can be restocked along the way at various grocery stores. Oftentimes, a good breakfast can be had in Canada for $4 or less in U.S. currency and makes an affordable treat to start the day off.

Long breaks are a good idea. And if you're driving up for the first time, I recommend taking more time to enjoy the sights. No matter where you're coming from, you will have to cross international borders. Be prepared for this and do your homework before you go. Find out exactly what is needed so there are no surprises. Keep your vehicle registration and driver's license handy, as well as identification for your children. Passports are also now required to pass through the Canadian border. Pets must have current rabies vaccinations and a health certificate available for inspection. Handguns are not allowed in Canada, but long rifles and shotguns may be transported across the border, which there may be a fee and/or registration for. Your belongings and vehicle might also be searched, including the contents of a trailer if you are hauling one. Sometimes you will actually be asked to park your vehicle and come inside, where you will be "run through" customs. Border agents might check your criminal background and ask questions.

One last thought about driving: Forget about that nice, smooth piece of glass you call a windshield. If it makes it through the journey without a crack or a chip you'll be lucky. Once you spend time in Alaska it's all but over anyway.

Resources for Your Trip North

Canada Border Services Agency (*www.cbsa-asfc.gc.ca/menu-e.html,*** click "Travellers")**

U.S. Customs (*www.customs.gov,*** click "Travel")**

Alaska Relocation (*www.labor.state.ak.us/research/relocate/relocmap.htm***)** This site will help you with everything you need to know about moving to Alaska, including the cost of living, community information, relocation analysis, employment opportunities, and more.

Bell's Alaska Travel Guide **(***www.bellsalaska.com***)** Indispensable guide for travel in British Columbia, the Yukon, and Alaska.

The Milepost **(***www.themilepost.com***)** The ultimate guide to road travel in the north, *The Milepost* has been advising travelers since 1949. This guidebook is packed with information, including gas prices, exchange rates, mileage calculators, trip-planning links, weather, history, and more. It also covers information about the ferry system and flying to Alaska and includes a pull-out map. This book is available at most bookstores and is worth its price in gold. It can also be ordered from their website, which is also worth checking out—lots of great information here.

Road Reports/Construction Advisories

In Alaska:

Alaska Department of Transportation and Public Facilities (*www.dot.state.ak.us*, click "Traveler Information"; the following Canadian sites can be accessed through this site as well)

In British Columbia:

Drive BC (*www.drivebc.ca*)

In the Yukon:

Yukon Department of Highways and Public Works (*www.gov.yk.ca/roadreport*)

Updated Travel Information: 5-1-1 (*http://511.Alaska.gov*)

This new system is slowly being implemented across the country. Statewide transportation agencies gather travel information regarding road closures, natural disasters affecting road travel, weather-related road conditions, traffic accidents, and more. This information is posted on the website, or can be accessed by dialing 511 within Alaska or 866-282-7577 from Outside.

FLOAT TO ALASKA

The Alaska Marine Highway Ferry System may well be the most relaxing way to reach Alaska. And the views just can't be beat. You will find lots of time to meet other travelers, catch up on a book, or just relax, as you may be on the ferry for two to four days depending on whether you board in Bellingham, Washington, or Prince Rupert, British Columbia. You can drive aboard, bike aboard, walk aboard, even board your kayak for the trip. Pets are allowed as well, but have to remain on the car deck. Sleeping quarters vary from a cabin berth to deck space where you pitch your tent in the open air. The solarium is a popular place to lounge, too. Lay out your sleeping bag on a lawn chair—orange heat lamps from above will keep you warm as the salty air breezes by, a wonderful feeling. Others simply find floor space inside or a reclining chair for sleeping. Showers are available as well.

Food is served cafeteria style and I'm convinced that the ferry system has the best navy bean and ham soup ever. The food in general is good and offers a nice variety. Plus, you can't complain about the view from your table! Snacks can also be purchased, and there's usually a bar or lounge for alcoholic beverages.

Road Recipe for Adventure

1 road to Alaska, crumbled

1 couple (*any brand*), stirred well

1 old truck, rusted

A fistful of dollars (*a dollop of American and a pinch of Canadian*)

2 hairy dogs (*optional*)

1 "gonna make a run for it" cat (*optional*)

3 spare tires

1 dim head light

1 stuck tape player

10 bologna sandwiches, at room temperature

A handful of bear sightings

2 flat tires

1 hot springs soak

2 border crossings

80 miles of road construction

1 windshield, cracked

2 speeding log trucks

A dash of "oh shits"

1 close call with a moose

3 bad arguments

2 wrong turns

7 days without a shower

½ a mind to turn around

1 Mix well.

2 Chill at 30 degrees Fahrenheit for 8 nights while sleeping under the dash.

3 Garnish with 4 gallons of road coffee.

4 Serve with a backache.

Yield: 2 grumpy, stinky travelers

One of the best things about the ferry is the wildlife you might see. The captain usually announces sightings of whales or perhaps sea lions resting on a buoy. You can almost feel the boat tip to one side as all the passengers crowd around the decks and windows to see. The scenery is also incredible, as the boat never ventures that far from shore, passing by islands and through inlets. Bald eagles are common, and if you're lucky, you might see a bear. A pair of binoculars is handy to have around.

If you have time to stop, it's worthwhile to visit some of the towns of the Southeast. For example, Ketchikan, Sitka, and Alaska's capital, Juneau, are showcases of local art, museums, Native culture, history, and the fishing industry. The Tongass National Forest covers much of the area, and a hike through the towering trees and lush vegetation is a spectacular way to spend the day. You could also charter a boat for fishing, rent a kayak—even get up close to a glacier if you wanted to. Just make sure to bring rain gear, as the Southeast has a notoriously wet climate. The patient visitor is rewarded when the sun appears and the clouds move out. The sights will take your breath away.

Ferry reservations are recommended, especially during the busy summer season. You may find that there is hardly any room for your sleeping bag, let alone your tent, during the peak tourist rush. But if driving the entire way to Alaska sounds too daunting, the ferry may be just your ticket. In the long run, it may cost more to take the ferry, but you will reach Haines or Skagway in a relaxed state and can begin your Alaskan adventure in short order from there—no matter your final destination.

All the information you need about the Alaska Marine Highway Ferry System can be found online (*www.dot.state.ak.us/amhs*). You can check the schedules and even make online reservations. *The Milepost* (*www.themilepost.com*) is also a good source of information concerning the ferry.

SIX REASONS YOU MIGHT CHANGE YOUR MIND ABOUT ALASKA

1 Seven months of winter

2 High suicide and alcoholism rates

3 Eagles prey on small pets

4 Can't find good coffee at the hardware store

5 You're a liberal vegetarian

6 You're allergic to two-cycle smoke

DIY

If you'd like to float to Alaska in your own personal boat, check out the books listed below. Travel by your lonesome (or twosome, etc.) is certainly possible and would make for a worthy adventure.

The Coastal Companion, by Joe Upton
Explore the Inside Passage mile by mile with this guide.

Exploring Southeast Alaska, **by Don Douglass and Reanne Hemingway-Douglass**

This guidebook boasts expert local knowledge, detailed anchor diagrams, GPS waypoints, and photographs. The authors' website (*www.fineedge.com*) also is packed with information for the Inside Passage boater, including maps, tide information, and links.

Row to Alaska By Wind and Oar, **by Pete and Nancy Ashenfelte**

A retired couple tells their story of an adventurous row up the Inside Passage.

Small Boat Cruising to Alaska, **by Leif G. Terdel**

This book covers planning, negotiating tides, currents, potential hazards, and places not to miss.

FLY TO ALASKA

Though not the most exciting way to go, flying is the fastest way to get to Alaska. It can also be affordable if you can be flexible about your schedule. Although you'll miss the excitement of an overland adventure, the time you will save may well be reason enough to fly. Look for deals in your local newspaper and take advantage of airline price wars, which can mean cheaper rates. Some online companies may also offer lower rates, so shop around if you've got the time. Here are some to look into:

- CheapTickets (*www.cheaptickets.com*)
- Expedia.com (*www.expedia.com*)
- Hotwire.com (*www.hotwire.com*)
- Priceline.com (*www.priceline.com*)

Airports in Alaska are much smaller and easier to navigate than those in the Lower 48 and show off the unique cross-section of folks coming and going—Alaska residents or not. Make sure to look for the characteristic Alaskan with luggage like coolers, cardboard boxes, or large plastic bins called ActionPackers wrapped with duct tape. Alaskan airports are generally safe enough to hole up in for a short while if needed—in the past I've felt comfortable enough to catch a couple hours of sleep on the floor with my backpack.

Regular airport amenities (food, gifts, etc.) are available in Anchorage, but substantially less so or nonexistent as you travel to smaller destinations.

Most of the bigger airports have rental cars available. Otherwise there are bus and shuttle services to get around the state. Bush flights to Alaska's smaller fly-in villages and backcountry are available almost everywhere.

One last advantage about flying: You can easily fly fresh fish home, as many local companies in the fishing ports are able to flash-freeze and vacuum-pack your catch for the ride home. Although the airline may charge you, it's a cheaper alternative than mailing your fish.

DIY

If you're really the adventurous type and want to fly to Alaska in your own plane, here are some resources to help you plan your trip.

Travel and Safety
Federal Aviation Administration (FAA)
222 W 7th Avenue #14
Anchorage, AK 99513-7587

Alaska Supplement (*www.naco.faa.gov/index.asp?xml=naco/catalog/charts/supplementary/supp_ak*)
Aeronautical chart from the FAA's National Aeronautical Charting Office, issued every fifty-six days. Includes an airport/facility directory, airport sketches, communications data, weather data sources, airspace information, listing of navigational facilities, and special notices and procedures.

Canada Flight Supplement (*www.fedpubs.com/mpchrt/charts/cfs.htm*)
Aeronautical chart from Natural Resources Canada, issued every fifty-six days, for planning and safe conduct of air operations. (Fee associated with obtaining this publication.)

Flight Tips for Pilots in Alaska (*www.alaska.faa.gov*)
There is some good general information here.

2

Finding Work:
How to *Really* Enjoy Alaska
and Get Paid (Barely)

If your idea of a good job includes subpar wages, boots covered by dog drool or fish slime, and the possibility of a predatory animal attack all the while having a great view out your "office" window, I've got good news—you're in the right place. Yeah, you could find a job here just like anywhere else in the Lower 48, but if you came up here for adventure, why settle for a "normal" job when you could have a job that pays much less for quadruple the fun? Why not be a dog handler, or a campground caretaker, or a fishing guide? That's what I'm talking about.

A CASE STUDY IN HOMESTEAD CARETAKING

I was not unlike most Alaskans in that I wanted to find my own place here. I wanted to find work that I enjoyed, land I could call my own, and adventures that I could recall when old and gray. When the notion of caretaking a homestead for the winter came about, I envisioned myself lounging around all winter sipping hot cocoa in my slippers and long johns. A break from working 9 to 5 would be nice. I thought of all the books I could read and the songs I could write. I'd make sourdough bread. I'd learn to play the fiddle. But unlike most Alaskans who knew better, my husband Dave and I took the job.

The homestead we would be caretaking was located at the very tip of the Alaska Peninsula directly across from the first Aleutian island—Unimak Island—and the village of False Pass. What follows are excerpts from my daily journal, with commentary (in italics) added in hindsight for clarification on what *really* was happening at the time.

Part I. Welcome to the Aleutians: This Is Your Life

Ah, a real chance to unwind and relax in a place as remote as they get. This was going to be a grand adventure! Everything seemed perfect and we were stoked.

September 15

We're on our way! I can't believe it. I'm so excited. We're held up in Cold Bay waiting for some weather to clear. Can't wait to see the homestead. Shouldn't be too long…This is a desolate place. *I thought Cold Bay was desolate? We'd dream about Cold Bay in a couple months, with its restaurant and liquor store and twenty or so people—and its liquor store…*

September 16

Arrived in the village yesterday after an exciting ride. My nose practically smeared the glass of the window beside me when the pilot banked our four-seater and spun us around for a better look at a brown bear walking along the beach. *I yelled "Yahoo!" but I was really trying not to vomit.*

We flew over the confluence of the Pacific Ocean and the Bering Sea and saw the beautiful treeless valleys, ridges, and mountains that the Aleutians are known for. *Waxing a bit poetically here—I was obviously not yet aware of the damage this treeless land would eventually inflict on our isolated psyches.* When we arrived, we were greeted by the owner of the homestead. As we were shaking hands a large unkempt man appeared from the other side of the rusted old van that would take us to the boat. We recognized him as the Swedish man we had heard about who had recently killed a bear that broke into his house for some salmonberry wine. He said he'd show us a picture. We had to travel about 3 miles across water to reach the homestead, which was nestled into a steep, rolling hillside. The waves and wind pounded us as we made our way in the 18-foot wooden skiff.

The place is set up to be totally self-sufficient, running on hydroelectric power from a nearby creek. To reach the house, you have to follow a narrow footpath that switchbacks about 100 yards up the hillside. Inside, there is an expansive pantry, and we were told that the supplies in the 5-gallon buckets along with the goods on the shelves could sustain the occupants for over a year or more. There was also as much canned and smoked fish as we could eat.

SEPTEMBER 17

The hillsides are covered with berries—salmonberries being the most prevalent. They're big but not a lot of flavor. *We would later pick about 5 gallons of these berries for wine, which we thoroughly enjoyed months later. It wasn't so much the taste...* The blueberries are the best—hard not to eat more than you pick. Have to watch out for bear. We carry a shotgun. The hiking is slow and steady—the moss being so spongy and deep. Ptarmigan flutter about in flocks. Their dog keeps humping my leg. I hate that dog.

SEPTEMBER 18

The last couple days we've been getting to know our caretaking duties. We were told that with rough winter weather, we had to be mindful to secure buildings and property so it wouldn't be destroyed or blown away in high winds. *I did not take this seriously.*

There are about fourteen chickens to take care of. Their coop is a small, rickety thing down by the greenhouse on the beach surrounded by barbed wire and regular chicken wire. There is brown bear hair on the barbs. The chickens will be fun I think. We'll have plenty of fresh eggs! *The chicken coop blew away during one of the first winter storms. Had to put the chickens in the greenhouse where they destroyed the entire contents within two days.*

SEPTEMBER 21

Made first coffee in days with a French press—mmmm good. I started a sourdough starter using potato puree. Went out in the skiff to look around and jig for halibut. Within a half hour I snagged a 70-pounder. We tried gaffing it about four times before finally getting a hold of it just as the jig broke free. I hugged the side of the boat when we flung it aboard to avoid the dangerous flopping. Amazing how strong they are. *We beat it to death.* Took a long time to clean and bag it. Cleaning that thing was like gutting a deer. *The only thing Dave caught was some unknown ocean creature that looked like a butt hole.*

SEPTEMBER 22

Went out in the skiff today to look for driftwood. That's the only way to get firewood here. We wrestle the logs in place and then hook up a rope from the skiff and tow them back to the homestead. The water was calm today, but we've seen it look pretty nasty already. *Like the Bermuda Triangle of the North.*

September 24

Calm, clear day today. Very low tide this morning. Found nice big limpets and decided to collect some for a stir-fry at lunch. We ended the day with a walk down the beach. Along the way, we saw something shiny floating just offshore but couldn't for the life of us figure out what it was. *Dave wished it was a beer.*

September 25

The homestead dog keeps starting fights with our dog. I wonder what we are going to do about him. *How 'bout he gets "lost"?*

October 1

The only heat in the house comes from the single burner on the old antique electric stove and the occasional firing of a water-jacket woodstove, which then radiates heat for a couple days afterwards. The house itself is very small—just a kitchen and small living area. Upstairs is the bedroom. The best thing about this place is the hot tub down on the beach. It is a wooden tub with a submerged woodstove on one side—good for bathing and soaking. *We would later get "trapped" by this hot tub one January night. See Chapter 5 for all the details...*

October 2

The chickens were entertaining tonight. One particular rooster stood at the top of the little chicken ramp with the feathers on his head all spiked from a freshwater bath. The peculiar way he cocked his head made him look like a chicken rock star.

October 3

Miserable gray day with winds and rain. Didn't eat much or do much. Feel sick. *Add on another 175 days and you've got yourself the quintessential Aleutian vacation.*

October 4

More rain and wind. Sourdough blueberry pancakes for breakfast were OK but lacking something. Nighttime rounds found gramma chicken dead in the coop! Don't want to eat her. *I'd regret that later.* Threw her in the sea.

OCTOBER 5

Rainy, windy, foggy. Gramma chicken washed back up on shore. Threw her out to sea again. *Same thing the next day.*

OCTOBER 7

There is a TV but it can only play videos, which we have none of, and the radio can't pick up any stations at all.

OCTOBER 8

Happy birthday to me! Saw a white wolf across the strait today. Finally got to really check out the pantry. *Lots of flour! Lots of rice! Love that tofu!* We have basic food supplies but have to be creative with recipes and mindful of not eating up all the good stuff at once. *Like ketchup and Velveeta.* We'll be eating lots of fish. *I now hate fish.* Made myself a chocolate cake. I got a wonderful homemade card.

OCTOBER 10

I've learned how to make really good sourdough English muffins. They are awesome with peanut butter. *We went through two gallons of peanut butter in seven months.*

Part II: A Fine Day for Carnivores

By now the reality of our plight had sunk in. We rarely had contact with the outside world and were subsisting on a diet of mainly fish and peanut butter. I was getting bloodthirsty. I was dreaming of hamburgers and steaks served in a busy restaurant by a very talkative waitress. My notes from the month of November all boiled down to the following entry in my journal.

NOVEMBER

All this fish is killing me. For the first couple weeks we thought, "Hey, this fish is just great, huh?" There was baked salmon, salmon patties, canned salmon, roasted salmon, deep-fried halibut, halibut spread, grilled halibut, and halibut cheeks. Be it frozen, fresh, canned, or smoked—we've had it. But the joy of eating fish has worn thin. Last night I woke Dave as I slept.

"Shoot 'em! Shoot 'em!"

"Honey, wake up!" he shouted. "You're dreaming!"

"Huh? Sorry. There was a flock of turkeys running through the living room."

"But you were chewing on my finger!"

"Oh, I'll try not to."

"Go back to sleep."

"Goodnight."

Of course we can purchase a small variety of things as needed in the tiny, two-aisle store in the village—including frozen meat. But since we haven't recently won the lottery, we won't be purchasing any "high-dollar" items—like meat. We have to wait for a caribou to come through the valley.

But I had another idea.

At first light the next morning I was outside with the shotgun to shoot me a ptarmigan. A light dusting of snow coated the ground as I made my way around the house and up the draw in the ravine. My mind wandered through recipes as I walked—roasted ptarmigan smothered in a light brown ginger sauce with wild rice, or maybe with ptarmigan gravy and mashed potatoes, or maybe I'd grill the breasts and then top them with a raisin-chutney glaze with sautéed green beans...WHOOSH! Right before my eyes a small flock took flight—wings beating as fast as the pounding of my heart. I wrestled the shotgun sling off my arm and brought it to my shoulder, catching it on my big sheepskin coat. But they were already gone. "Aw—aw damn!" I raised my fist and extended my middle finger to the white birds as they climbed higher and higher, settling into a twisted maze of alders a half mile away.

Shortly after my hunting expedition, we took the skiff over to the village and I found myself standing in front of the chest freezer in the store. I opened the lid and looked inside. There were frozen T-bones, a ham, pork chops, hamburger, sausage.

I glanced back at the T-bone and its price: $31.95. I felt like one of those cartoon characters when their heads enlarge, eyes bug out, jaw drops to the floor, and a sort of "Aahhooogaaa" sound comes out. I quietly closed the lid and opened the one next to it. Nothing but ice cream, frozen pizzas, frozen burritos, and frozen dinners. My mouth watered. It all looked wonderful.

"Doritos, maybe there's some Doritos here somewhere," I mumbled aloud. Closing the freezer lid, I looked around the store. I could almost taste that artificial cheese dust caked on my fingertips. There were no

Doritos. I slinked up to the counter with two cans of beets and leaned against it.

"You 'bout ready, hun?" Dave asked.

My ravaged eyes glanced back at the freezer, so close I could kick it.

"Yep," I sighed. "I guess I'm ready."

I bought a stale Halloween candy bar for two bucks.

It isn't like we are starving. There is at least a year's supply of food in the pantry, including all the beans and rice a person could eat (don't try and stop me!) and flour and pancake mix and tea and potatoes and eggs—and don't forget about fish! The homestead, after all, is nestled amidst some of the best commercial fishing grounds in the entire world. Like it or not, fish is our main course.

Winter is beginning to take hold. Still no caribou. Next visit to the store, I noticed that Dave seemed edgy, distorted, weak. I knew exactly what he needed. I ran to the freezer, opened the lid and grabbed two packages of hamburger. A laugh gurgled from my deepest being. A pirate-esque demeanor was overcoming me. HA, HA! I've got you now! I hobbled with my peg-leg to the counter, handed over some gold, and then stuffed the meat into the treasure chest on our waiting ship.

The skiff ride back was really pleasant, even though we had just spent our last twenty bucks. When the first patty hit the cast iron skillet atop the woodstove, the sweet smell of sweaty grease choked the air and filled the house. We were giddy. We sliced a piece of our revered Velveeta cheese for each person and I sautéed an onion too. After toasting some home-made sourdough English muffins, we slathered each side with mayonnaise and sliced our last jarred pickle. With some homemade yogurt, I prepared a ranch chip-dip using some spices and declared it the "best ever"—although it just tasted like spiced yogurt. From the pantry, I grabbed one of our last bags of all-natural, baked potato slices, and returned to the kitchen with the excitement of a kid at Christmas. When our burgers were ready, we sat down for a prayer. It was quicker than normal.

We sat in silence with grease dripping from our chins and down our wrists, smiling. There was no need for conversation, really.

"Tastes just like a restaurant," I exclaimed with my mouth full.

"Uh-huh," Dave grunted.

"Good chip dip, eh?"

"Yeah, it's great."

We stuffed our faces slowly and deliberately.

"I think the first caribou we see is in serious trouble," I said, already canning it in my mind.

"I think we should sneak over and get one of those wild cows," Dave said smiling.

Oddly enough, there is said to be a herd of wild cows on the first Aleutian island.

"Do you want another one?" Dave asked as he got up to heat up the skillet.

"Oh yeah," I answered.

We didn't eat anything for the rest of the day. Protein overload. I did whip up a wicked batch of snow ice cream topped with hot cocoa powder though. Maybe we'll survive this yet...

Part III: The Mirage of Sanity

Our lives, meat-deprived as they were, would soon get much worse. The isolation of the winter months wiped out any sense of adventure we had left and locked us inside the small, lukewarm house for weeks on end. We were running out of fuel for the generator, wood for the stove, had read every book in the house, and were longing for stunt doubles. Only long delirious days of Yahtzee and an airplane delivery of liquor would save us now.

JANUARY 9

We are now locked in by ice. The entire pass is filled with icebergs 7 to 8 feet thick and as big as football fields. Wind chill 35 below—temperature 10. We haven't got mail since December 23. I put some dried salmon outside in hopes that a fox or weasel would come by to munch on it so we could stare out the window at wild animals like we were at the zoo. The dogs found it.

JANUARY 10

Weather forecast—blizzard. Back down to 59 in the house. We're not sure but we might be out of gas for the generator. Today the wind is gusting harder than I think I've ever seen it. We are out of onions, flour, and almost out of coffee. *Oh, hell.* There's plenty to eat. There is canned salmon, smoked salmon *(I want to kill myself)*, halibut, applesauce, and salmonberry jelly. We still have some pasta and canned pumpkin.

January 13

Blizzard. It was 53 in the house this morning, probably in the 30s upstairs. I have on two pairs of long underwear. One is falling apart. I sleep in my clothes. We have four sticks of butter left. Snuck up on some otters today. I could lean all of my weight into the wind and it held me up.

February 8

I'm a little worried about Dave—I think he's had enough of this place. Today is his birthday. He just moped around all day and didn't say much. We've still got three months to go. I tempted him with a can of peaches but couldn't cheer him up and finally just let him sulk.

February 27

Played Yahtzee for nine hours today. We were playing to see who did dishes. I don't remember who won.

March 2

We just ordered $200 worth of liquor from Cold Bay. Should arrive on the mail plane in a couple days. I got a box of wine and a fifth of Jim Beam. Dave got a fifth of tequila and some blackberry brandy. Shipping was around $40.

March 8

HA, HA! It's liquor day!

March 16

Went sledding on a hill behind the house. We used an old sled we found in the shed. On one run down Dave tore up his leg pretty good on a pipe sticking out of the ground...A PIPE! We're in the middle of nowhere. WHY IS THERE A ****ING PIPE STICKING OUT OF THE GROUND!! Otherwise it was a pretty nice day.

April 12

We're gonna have a party. We're just about out of wood so we figure we'll burn up the rest in a fire on the beach. Sort of a cleansing thing. Our salmonberry wine is ready and tastes great. *It tasted like diesel.* Blazing ball of eye poison is out today so we figure we'll take advantage of it. *I'm referring to the sun here.* Dave found a cigar. I wish he'd find some drugs.

April 13

Salmonberry wine is gone and I can hardly move today. I think I heard wolves howling last night. My teeth hurt. Eggs for lunch and dinner. Didn't get up for breakfast. Probably would have had eggs.

April 28

We just saw the first ferry of the year go by on its way to Dutch Harbor. Oh—I can just picture the cozy chairs and a movie playing and food—lots of good cafeteria food! Dave just made some comment about getting out of this "hell hole." Somebody's in a bad mood…

May 4

We're outta here. Nobody died.

And there's the whole, wonderful "event," as we like to call it. We flew out about a week later and went straight to Arby's. Although, flying back to Anchorage was a bit of a culture shock for sure. The traffic was something else.

Epilogue

Looking back, the whole experience wasn't that bad. Of course it's easy to say that months or years after the actual event, but I still think I would do it again. For me, it was a time for expression and an exercise in creativity. I wrote an entire album's worth of songs, wrote stories, and really just kept myself constantly busy with projects. If I had to do it again, I would pick a different location, though. Somewhere with trees and more large animals to kill for meat—somewhere in the Interior or Brooks Range. A fishing lodge in the Southeast would be nice too.

My husband, on the other hand, was much more affected by the isolation. He would not do it again. Seven months is a long time to be so isolated. You can make all the plans in the world, but you can't act on them until you're out of there, and that really got to him. All in all, it was an adventure we will never forget.

This Could Be You Too

If you're still reading, I'm assuming you want to know how to land a caretaking job like this yourself.

Check the newspapers. Start looking in August and you may come up with a lead. The Anchorage and Fairbanks papers are your best bet.

Subscribe to *The Caretaker Gazette*, a bimonthly publication that lists hundreds of jobs throughout the world and occasionally lists some Alaskan opportunities. That's how we learned of our gig. I actually called the publisher before the next issue was out to see if any Alaska jobs were listed. They gave me the information early, and lucky for us, that helped us be the first to apply for the job. Take note though: most employers want to hire someone who's already in the state and has a bit of remote experience. Not always, but they want to make sure you won't freak out come January when you've just read the last book in sight and you're out of hot cocoa.

Call wilderness lodges directly. This is a bold move, but if you really want a caretaking job, this may take you just where you want to go. Search the Internet for remote hunting/fishing/wilderness lodges in Alaska and see what you come up with. It's worth a try.

Anchorage Daily News
PO Box 149001
Anchorage, AK 99514-9001
In Alaska: 800-478-4200
Outside: 907-257-4200
www.adn.com

The Caretaker Gazette
PO Box 4005-M
Bergheim, TX 78004
830-336-3939
www.caretaker.org
caretaker@caretaker.org

Fairbanks Daily News-Miner
PO Box 70710
Fairbanks, AK 99707
907-456-6661
www.news-miner.com

Homer Tribune
601 E Pioneer Avenue #109
Homer, AK 99603-7142
907-235-3714
www.homertribune.com

Juneau Empire
3100 Channel Drive
Juneau, AK 99801
907-586-3740
www.juneauempire.com

Kodiak Daily Mirror
1419 Selig Street
Kodiak, AK 99615
907-486-3227
www.kodiakdailymirror.com

Ketchikan Daily News
501 Dock Street/PO Box 7900
Ketchikan, AK 99901
907-225-3157
www.ketchikandailynews.com

Peninsula Clarion
PO Box 3009
Kenai, AK 99611
907-283-7551
www.peninsulaclarion.com

VOLUNTEER OPPORTUNITIES

Besides our stint as caretakers for the homestead, we've also found work as campground hosts with the Alaska State Parks Volunteer Program. Although for some positions you need an RV or camper trailer to be a host, there are plenty of places that provide housing and other amenities. These positions can be found all over the state, and not only can you become a caretaker for a campground or facility, you can work as trail crew, a ranger assistant, a natural-history interpreter, or even as a winter park caretaker. These positions are open to those eighteen and older, with no upper age limit. If you're looking for college credit, internships are also available.

The nice thing about one of these seasonal posts is the chance to experience a part of Alaska before you actually set down roots. It's a nice way to check out the climate, people, recreation, and opportunities of that area. If, on the other hand, you want to make money, avoid these positions like the plague. But if you've got some time to burn, a book to write, or just want to let your hair grow out, these positions really work. Deadline for summer applications is April 1; winter applications, October 1.

For the Alaska State Parks Volunteer Program Catalog

Volunteer Coordinator
Alaska State Parks
550 W 7th Avenue, Suite 1380
Anchorage, AK 99501-3561
907-269-8708
907-269-8907 (fax)
volunteer@dnr.state.ak.us

For Applications and Volunteer Listings

Alaska Department of Natural Resources (*www.dnr.state.ak.us/parks/vip/index.htm*)

WORKING IN THE FISHING INDUSTRY

Many an Alaskan's first job is working in the fishing industry. You may have heard stories about working the "slime line" in canneries and how you can't get that smell out of your clothes...Anyway, whether it's a cannery job you seek, or you want to experience the adventure of charter fishing as a deck hand, you'll find plenty of options here in Alaska. You don't need experience for many of the jobs.

Below are some resources to get you started on your job hunt. Some fishing employment sites charge fees to gain access to the job information listed. They may be worth checking out for general information or as a last resort if you're desperate for work. Check Alaska's Job Bank first and try contacts through that site for the information you need.

AlaskaJobFinder.com (*www.alaskajobfinder.com*)
Job listings for canneries, commercial fishing boats, and processing facilities; $3.95 for a five-day subscription, $12.95 for a thirty-day subscription.

Alaska's Job Bank (*www.jobs.state.ak.us*)
Click on "Seafood Jobs in Alaska" for free job listings, information, and links about fishing jobs.

JobMonkey.com (*www.jobmonkey.com/alaska*)
JobMonkey.com's Alaska jobs section is in partnership with AlaskaJobFinder. com, but you may find useful tips here about the industry.

Seafood Employment Hotline
From Anchorage or Outside: 907-269-4770, ext. 7
From rural Alaska: 800-473-0688

HUNTING/FISHING GUIDE

Alaska is known for its hunting and fishing opportunities. People come from all over the world to experience its bounties. Think you'd like to become a hunting or fishing guide? These agencies will help you figure out if you've got what it takes.

Hunting Guides

Big Game Commercial Services Board Licensing Authority
Alaska Department of Community and Economic Development
Division of Occupational Licensing, Big Game Guide and
Transporter Licensing Section
PO Box 110806
Juneau, AK 99811-0806
907-465-2543
www.dced.state.ak.us/occ/pgui.htm
Information on licensing, applications, regulations, fees, and exams.

Commercial Sport-Fishing Guides

Alaska Division of Fish and Game
Sport Fishing Guide Program
333 Raspberry Road
Anchorage, AK 99578
907-267-2369
www.sf.adfg.state.ak.us/statewide/guides/guide.cfm
Information, regulations, and registration.

DOG MUSHER

Much of Alaska is at least a little bit dog crazy—except maybe for the Southeast, where they get more rain than snow in the winter. After all, dogsledding is our state sport.

Becoming a dog musher is like getting a cavity. It comes on sort of slow and then WHAM! You've got thirty dogs in your backyard and the doctor tells you it's serious: "Yep, you're a dog musher." Which is a lot like being a dairy farmer, which means you can't go anywhere and you gotta take out a second mortgage just to feed the beasts, but heck it sure will make you happy. If you really want to go for broke, you race those dogs. Check out these sources to help you get started, find mentors, register for races, and more.

Alaska Dog Mushers Association
PO Box 70662
Fairbanks, AK 99707
907-457-MUSH
adma@sleddog.org
www.sleddog.org
Sponsors the International Sled Dog Symposium held in Fairbanks every October. The weekend-long event features guest speakers, how-to demonstrations, a trade show, and information about all things related to dog mushing.

Dogsled.com (*www.dogsled.com*)
Their motto is "All of the adventure, none of the frostbite."

Mushing Magazine
PO Box 149
Ester, AK 99723
907-479-0454
info@mushing.com
www.mushing.com
"The Magazine of Dog-Powered Adventure." Information for both professional and recreational dog mushers, including dog care, technique, racing, and more.

Sled Dog Central (*www.sleddogcentral.com*)
Online sled dog source for advertising and other information.

DOG HANDLER

So you'd rather help on the sidelines than admit to a full-blown case of "I want to be a dog musher"? That's fine, and probably a smart thing to do to find out if you like the work and commitment it takes to be a dog musher proper. First, you've got to find a dog musher that needs help. Usually these are the mushers that run the bigger races and have a substantial amount of dogs to take care of and train. You might get room and board in exchange for helping to run the dogs, care for the dogs, clean up after the dogs, etc. Most times you might get a small stipend too. Then come race time, you'll follow the musher around and assist him or her on and off the trail. How do you find these jobs? Here are some ideas:

- Word of mouth. Ask around at places where mushers hang out (feed stores, races, Laundromat, etc.).
- Check the classifieds.
- Listen to the local radio classifieds programs.
- Post a wanted ad in the paper, at the Laundromat, feed stores, etc.

COOL JOBS

If you're looking for adventurous work in the great Alaskan outdoors, CoolWorks (*www.coolworks.com/alaska-jobs*) has it all, including lodge/resort jobs, jobs on the water, National Park Service jobs, ski resort jobs, internships, and land tour jobs. Check it out.

EVERYTHING ELSE

If you're looking for mainstream jobs, by far the best website for Alaskan jobs is Alaska's Job Bank (*www.jobs.state.ak.us*), through the State of Alaska website. The job postings are listed by region, and after registering you can easily access all the information there, which is updated frequently. You'll also find information about state government jobs, job fair calendars, apprenticeships, veteran services, job training, Alaska job centers, and more.

Powered by Enthusiasm

Kathy Leninger, a thirty-year veteran of dog mushing, is as passionate about the sport as anyone I have ever met. She exudes the spirit of wanderlust and adventure that Alaska is known for through her tales of mushing dogs for a living. And her physical strength and stature belies the fact that this fifty-something woman is the single mother of two.

Kathy's East Coast family thought she was crazy when, after obtaining a degree in psychology and fine art, she moved up to Alaska all those years ago to find adventure in a wilderness she could only vaguely imagine. Her first attempt at mushing was a learning experience. The sled was too small and the dogs were untrained and unruly, but when things went right she was in awe of the quiet power and the awesome feeling of being connected to the land. She was hooked.

Kathy has been running dogs for a living ever since. She has helped run and train dogs for other kennels, mushed tourists into the wilderness for day- and week-long adventures, and has her own business offering visitors short rides with her dogs.

Kathy admits the life of a dog musher is tough. The expenses are outrageous—dog food alone is a huge drain on your wallet unless you live where fish is readily available. She is always grateful for the donation of a dead horse to supplement her dog food supply. Then there are shots, worming, harnesses, booties, chains, dog houses, straw—you get the picture. Just taking care of them is a full-time job. And there can be dangers—like falling through ice on a lake (this happened to Kathy and her dogs pulled her out to safety), or being dragged by your team (you may lose them if you let go), or encountering a moose.

Mushers often have to supplement their income with other jobs. In the summer Kathy sometimes leases her dogs to a company that offers tourists dog-sled rides on a glacier in Seward. "You do whatever you can," she says. But ultimately, her heart lies in dog mushing. And there is no doubt—as her voice absolutely radiates with excitement when she talks about it.

When asked what words of wisdom she would give to those wanting to be a dog musher, she offered the following:

- Visit kennels and find a mentor. Figure out if you really want to do it.
- Remember, dogs aren't disposable.
- Make sure you love it.
- What any dog lacks in speed, it will give you in heart.

Although Kathy has raced dogs in the past, she is happiest running dogs with tourists in tow. Working with tourists is a more laid-back venture. They don't really care how fast they go, they just want that connection to the earth—a break from their harried city lives—and that brings Kathy enormous satisfaction.

Kathy currently owns seventeen dogs. She harbors no fantasies about getting rich or living an easy life. She simply enjoys the thrill and serenity of standing on sled runners while her dogs lead her through the quiet world of winter's beauty. For her there is nothing better.

There is work to be found no matter where you go in Alaska. You might have to get a bit creative at times, but persistence pays off. No matter what, you'll probably come away with a good story.

3

Coffee, Carhartts, and Cabin Living: How to *Be* an Alaskan

You can usually pick an Alaskan out of a crowd. Carhartts, wool shirts, and beaver hats are the norm—and that's just the women. We shop at places called the Prospector, Big Ray's, and Rugged Gear and Work Store. We are obsessed with coffee. There are nearly as many espresso stands in Alaska as there are dogs—another one of our obsessions. And you'll never truly be considered an Alaskan until you've lived in a cabin without running water and endured outhouses at 30 below. Read on to learn how to graduate from cheechako to sourdough.

I WAS BORN TO LOOK LIKE THIS

I think I was always meant to be an Alaskan. In Alaska, you don't have to keep up with current fashion trends or stay alert to what the hip crowd is doing. No, in fact many cute outfits that look good elsewhere just look like you're trying too hard here. I was subject to this opinion the other day when I wore a miniskirt with leggings (supposed to be in style right now—saw it in the local grocery flyer) and some construction workers laughed at me. I thought I was looking good, you know, looking hip. That's when I realized my mistake: I had the wrong shoes! It's bunny boots *before* Memorial Day and then mukluks until Labor Day. I had it switched! Oh, staying haute-couture is so trying! (But really, construction workers would know.)

So I don't have the greatest fashion sense. What I do have is a good pair of work pants, and every woman in Alaska has at least three pairs of these. The first pair is the grimiest pair, used for chain-saw work, peeling logs, hauling manure to the garden, and scooping dog poop. The second pair is not so full of holes but is covered with paint and various stains from the constant "work in progress" that is her house. The third pair is for going out to social events that at once say "I'm a hard working Alaskan woman" and "the nearest fashion mall is hundreds of miles from here."

This does not affect most men's opinions that Alaskan woman are beautiful. Although, if Carhartt ever came up with a line of summer halter dresses or lingerie for women, I think Alaskan men would be thrilled.

On a whim the other day I bought some mascara. I don't know what I was thinking. Maybe I was having one of those blue days we women have after becoming acutely aware of our crow's-feet cracked eyes, expanding midsections, and innate ability to grow a mustache (isn't that hilarious). So it hit me. "Hey, how about some mascara to cheer you up!" So off I went to the nearest grocery store to check it out. I found "ultra-lash," "superstar lash," "supersexy superstar lash," and the store brand mascara, which just said, "You found me and I'm cheap." Jackpot. I threw it in my cart and suddenly felt better. I was a woman shopping for makeup.

I rushed home and put on my best dress work pants and gingerly applied my new identity. Then I went out and worked in the garden. It must be true that makeup makes you feel beautiful, because I was soon waving at every four-wheeler that passed our place.

My husband got home and saw me in a different light too. "Wow, look at you!" he said. "Yeah," I said smiling.

As he gently wiped the hair from my eyes he said, "You've got dead mosquitoes squished all over your face!"

TWELVE SIMPLE WAYS TO LOOK THE PART

OK, so you made it to Alaska and now you need to fit in. How do you do that? Well, you need to look like an Alaskan. I polled at least three Alaskans to help shuffle through all the dos and don'ts, and here's their advice.

RULE #1:

Don't wear a suit. In fact if you own a suit, now's a good time to throw it into the woodstove where it belongs. You're gonna need all the heat you can get 'cause winters can be cold. If you do wear a suit and go out in public, you will stop traffic and people will point and laugh. Unless it's

Halloween. Then they'll just think it's a crummy costume. Cancel that if you work for the government. People will swear at you. So go get yourself a woodstove if you don't have one and start chopping wood already.

Rule #2:

You probably won't go swimming much but you *will* vacation in Hawaii, so don't throw out that swimsuit yet. There are almost 700,000 Alaskans in this state and at least most of them have been to Hawaii. That's why you see so many beautiful paper leis hanging from rearview mirrors. Another reason to hang onto that swimsuit is because there are often parties in the winter that will attempt to lull you into a false sense of a warm climate, complete with tropical dress code and umbrella drinks. Don't be fooled, but do be festive.

Rule #3:

Showers and clean clothes are overrated. In other parts of the country, it's considered uncouth to skip a daily shower. In an effort to be unlike the rest of the country, we skip the couth. We wouldn't know couth unless it was a species of fish and it hit us in the head while we were ending its life with a rock. Some of us don't have running water and instead haul every drop in 5-gallon containers or in tanks in the back of our trucks. For this reason, water for drinking and cooking tends to trump daily showers and clean clothes. Some well-meaning Lower 48ers once commented on my husband's choice of clothing as he was leaving for the grocery store: "Are you going to wear that?" I was stunned. Huh? We are talking about Fairbanks here, right? He wasn't bloody from dressing out a moose or anything. He just had on his everyday "might need to change a tire or cut some wood or pour some concrete" type of clothes. And yeah, they might have been a bit dirty. And yes, oddly, he was carrying a briefcase (it was a work day). But come on! If Alaska turns into the kind of place where you have to clean up to go to the grocery store, well, stamp my forehead and send me to Canada.

Rule #4:

Fur is warm. Yes, I said it. Don't be afraid to wear fur. Now, I'm not advocating that the whole state take up trapping, but it is a fact of life here. And man, fur will keep you warmer than anything else you'll ever wear.

Animals seem to do just fine with it. Beaver hats and mitts are priceless. Wolf ruffs are the stuff for parka hoods. Wear a big old fur hat in New York and you'll get laughed off the street or get paint thrown at you. Wear the same hat in Alaska and people will stop and ask you if you made it yourself and tell you how beautiful it is. And on the subject of keeping warm, bunny boots are the best. No bunnies are killed in the making of these wonderful rubber military boots and you will be fashionably Alaskan when you wear them. Mukluks are also quite warm and are again appropriate at the grocery store, church, or outings to your favorite restaurant. It's OK to dress warm here. Unlike other hip places where it's more important to look cool than be warm, in Alaska it's suicide to be hip.

Rule #5:

Buy stock in Carhartts. I know our state flag is blue with an image of the Big Dipper and the North Star in blazing yellow, but the real symbol of Alaska should be a ragged pair of Carhartts flying on a flagpole above the state capitol. Consider this: there are at least three Carhartt Balls around the state where folks actually gather together to showcase the gnarliest, dirtiest, ripped-up Carhartts they can find in their wardrobes. This is the required attire for the evening. Folks also tell stories of how their Carhartts supposedly saved their lives in one way or another. Prizes are given. Marriages are proposed. Alaska is proud.

Rule #6:

If you're going to settle in the Southeast, get a pair of XTRATUFs, also called Sitka Slippers. These are very supple, calf-high, brown rubber boots that will become permanently attached to your feet. They are very comfortable—thus the name Sitka Slippers. And don't forget to tuck your pant legs into the boots. On the subject of footwear, mostly coastal Alaskans, but many Alaskans in general, wear an ankle-high leather slip-on shoe with a smooth sole. There's even a tab above the heel to help you slip them on. Very comfortable. You will also need some Grundens or Helly Hansen rain gear to keep you dry—preferably bibs with a coat—especially if you're going to be working in the fishing industry. A nice short wool cap will keep your lid warm in all that rain and will keep you looking like a coastal Alaskan.

Rule #7:

Makeup is optional. There is a lot of natural beauty in Alaska and its women are no exception. This state attracts a lot of the rugged outdoor type, the type that doesn't need additives or preservatives. Or makeup. Makeup on the men is frowned upon.

Rule #8:

Embrace the hippie culture. Yes, there are lots of hippies in Alaska. Old hippies, new hippies, musical, artsy, political, happy hippies. They still look the same as they did yesterday. Handmade wool sweaters on the men, gauzy, flowing skirts on the women. Long hair, all. Earthy. Patchouli oil. Hemp handbags and jewelry. Coffeehouse regulars. You get the picture. Be free, dress like a hippie.

Rule #9:

Duct tape. It is handy for everything including rips on pants, coats, boots, and all in between. If you want to look like an Alaskan, slap some duct tape on your clothes or your gear.

Rule #10:

Put a Leatherman or other type of multitool on your belt.

Rule #11:

If you *don't* want to look like an Alaskan, by all means, go out and buy some new hiking boots, bright Gore-Tex rain gear, and a Cabela's safari hat. And dress identical to your spouse. That's it in a nutshell. Alaskans look like they live here. Visitors just look too coordinated and put together to really live here. They don't have the look of long cold winters, dead car batteries, smoking woodstoves, or endless coastal rain on their faces. They look happy. That's what you get when life's too easy—when you don't have to worry about not being the highest member of the food chain. When you don't have to worry about freezing to death if you break down or haven't slept in weeks because the dang sun won't set. That's just a bonus when you become an Alaskan. You just look the part automatically.

LAST RULE:

It's Alaska. Do what you want. Dress how you want. And when someone asks how long you've lived here, lie and tell them at least five years. That's what we all did.

BECOMING THE ALASKAN WOMAN

Being a woman in Alaska isn't easy. It's cold, the produce is bad, and a lot of times your best shopping bet is the hardware store. There are lots of manly men out there, but they don't seem to be much help. Most of them are a little preoccupied with the next hunting season or with getting a bigger TV. Then for Valentine's Day they get you cold-weather gear. Some are just plain crazy—and there are a lot of crazies. I would never advise against moving to Alaska, but I hear Iowa is nice too.

The Alaska life really isn't that bad. Before you know it, you'll have your very own mountain man and you'll be able to start a fire with one match. In any case, here's some advice I wish someone had given me:

1 I know it's Alaska, but hairy armpits aren't cool anywhere.

2 You must learn how to navigate triple-layered children at 20 below.

3 You must learn patience when these same children ask to use the bathroom.

4 The giant cabbage contests are just for *fun*.

5 Being able to butcher a moose is a skill that will get you a date.

6 All the cake in the world won't make the winters shorter.

7 You're only fooling yourself if you buy a swimsuit in Alaska.

8 If you're having a bad day, remember, it's colder in Antarctica.

9 You will come to realize that flannel and wool wear well.

10 You will learn to love the smell of wet dogs.

BECOMING THE ALASKAN MAN

It's not easy being a man in Alaska. The women expect you to be able to keep them safe, warm, and happy. And Lord knows that last one is a doozy. There's only so much of you to go around and too little time for hunting, fishing, snow-machining, and the sports channel. Then there's Valentine's Day, and it's either make or break with those new gloves you got her. And sometimes, if it wasn't so hard to find a good woman in Alaska, you'd just as soon go back to living alone in a small cabin with your dogs. But you've grown really fond of her little smelly soaps and candles she has everywhere. And she's pretty good at start-ing a fire when you go camping. Alaska women aren't so bad, you just have to know how to play your cards. Here's what you need to know about becoming a man in Alaska:

1 Your Carhartts won't wash themselves.

2 Rest assured, you can get cable in Alaska.

3 Don't kid yourself. We all know your wife is not to blame for that new truck. Or that camper. Or the four-wheeler.

4 Save that big fur hat and those bunny boots for your second date.

5 Sometimes, your best bet might be to lie and tell the woman you have a place in Hawaii.

6 A new fishing boat will only impress your buddies.

7 Don't worry, guns go on sale around dividend time.

8 Once in a while, you should make your dog team sleep on the floor.

9 Two words: LINT BRUSH.

10 If you came to Alaska expecting to find a woman who likes the cold, can filet a fish, and looks good in a dress, you're on the right track. But that one's already married and has a gun.

CABIN LIVING

Cabin living is a definitive part of becoming an Alaskan. It just wouldn't be right to exist in this state without first living without water and using an outhouse at

30 below. It just helps you earn your stripes and will give you a real taste of the fabled Last Frontier. Then if you do graduate to a bona fide modern existence, your appreciation for a hot shower in your own home will be at least tripled.

THE OUTHOUSE AND YOU: A GUIDE

An outhouse is a personal thing—from what kind of decorations you hang to the kind of toilet paper you use. But some things are just plain smart.

- **Put your toilet paper in a waste basket so the hole doesn't fill up as fast (a paper bag works well, and then you can burn it).**

- **Make sure to position your outhouse so you'll have a nice view while sitting.**

- **Long parkas work well for keeping your legs warm while sitting in the winter.**

- **You'll want to keep some kind of stick or shovel nearby to knock over the**

First, let's talk about acquiring land. The last time you could get land for free in Alaska was in 1986, at which point the Homesteading Act was retired. Free land is no longer an option, although there are yearly land auctions through the Bureau of Land Management and the Department of Natural Resources. These auctions are usually for parcels of land less than 10 acres and that, if not sold at auction, are then available for sale over the counter. Much of this land is remote and/or recreational, but still may be worth looking into. To find out more, check out the Department of Natural Resources' land offerings (*www.dnr.state.ak.us/mlw/landsale*) or the Alaska Mental Health Trust Land Office (*www.mhtrustland.org*). If you are considering building your own cabin you must first determine if your land contains permafrost. Permafrost is defined as "ground that remains frozen for two years or more." Much of the Interior and some of Southcentral Alaska contains permafrost soils that will wreak havoc on buildings if built improperly. If you build your cabin directly on a foundation or concrete slab on permafrost soils, within time, you will find it sinking or tilting from thawing ground as your cabin heats up the area underneath it. It will eventually make the structure crooked at best, and unsafe at worst.

If you are curious about whether or not your land contains permafrost, look to the trees for a clue. Stunted black spruce with not much else growing is usually a sign of underlying permafrost. If it takes you two weeks to dig a sufficient outhouse hole because you can only dig a little bit each day as the air thaws the exposed soil, then it's a good bet you have permafrost issues. You can also pay to have a core sample of your soil extracted to determine for sure if you have permafrost on your land.

In order to build on permafrost, you need to build on what is called a post-and-pad foundation. This means the structure sits completely off the ground on elevated concrete pillars or wooden timbers, which in turn sit on "concrete cookies" placed on top of the ground. As yearly shifting occurs, each pillar can be shimmed or adjusted as needed to maintain a level building.

Since land with permafrost is not ideal for building, it can be cheaper than land with soils that will accommodate a large house with a foundation and a drilled well. And this brings me to the most talked about issue of cabin living—running water. Or the lack thereof. Drilling for a well in permafrost soils is not cost efficient and not practical. Most cabin dwellers must haul their own water from wells around town that are used specifically for this purpose. Some folks get their water delivered by a water truck and will go through 100–1000 gallons a month if they have a plumbed water tank. That's a real luxury and makes the hassle of hauling water almost nonexistent. For others, their 5-gallon containers sit on the edge of the kitchen sink, which drains down to a 5-gallon bucket, which in turn must be emptied when full.

You'd be surprised how conservation-oriented you become when you must physically handle every drop of water you use. You get good at taking baths out of large kettles warmed on the stove—with a gallon or so of water. Rinse water from dishes becomes water for the garden or the houseplants. You start to use a lot of wet wipes even if you don't have small children.

"poopcicle" that will grow in the winter like an upside down stalactite—except not as cool.

- A foam seat is a must in the winter.

- If you add a little bit of lime occasionally to the hole, it won't smell as bad.

- Install a vent from the bottom of your outhouse to the outside using a smoke stack. This too will keep the stink out.

- Two-holers are OK to look at, but really, you'll never want to take a friend in there with you.

And then a funny thing happens. You get used to it. You don't mind not taking showers every day—you even start enjoying it. You start collecting water from the roof during the summer and love it when it rains. You set up a solar shower outside and look forward to that refreshing blast of warm water while standing naked in the trees. Yes, you are a cabin dweller and can take care of yourself. And it feels good.

Then nature calls, and it's so cold that a cup of hot water thrown into the air crystallizes before it hits the ground. No matter how you look at it, your bare backside will eventually have to face the cold, hard truth of your outhouse. Go to the nearest hardware store and buy a piece of 1-inch blue foam board, the kind used to insulate houses—that's what you need for a toilet seat. You're also going to need an empty coffee can with a lid for your toilet paper. This will keep your paper dry in addition to keeping the squirrels from turning it into confetti. Next, you'll need a magazine rack for summer reading and maybe even a candle you can light in the winter. If you want to get really fancy, you could add a heater powered by an extension cord from the house. You can kick it on a few minutes before venturing forth and, boy, what a cozy place that will be. OK, maybe "cozy" sets the wrong tone for this subject, but you get the idea. I also like to add Christmas lights on the same extension cord for an added bit of festiveness. That doesn't sound right either, but heck, nobody said cabin dwellers had to be dull. Memorabilia from various trips you've taken, such as postcards and maps, make for good outhouse decoration too, as do your favorite cartoons and sayings. Photos of loved ones aren't recommended. A hanging scented tree usually rounds out my list of outhouse necessities. You want it to smell as good as an outhouse can when you have guests over.

Of course, there's an alternative to enduring the frigid outhouse even if you don't have indoor plumbing. And that's the honey bucket—the rarely talked about, but closet secret (literally) of many a cabin dweller. A honey bucket is simply a 5-gallon pail outfitted with a toilet seat in which you can do your business in the warmth of your own cabin. Then, it can be emptied as needed into the outhouse. I've gone so far as to build a nice varnished wooden box that fits nicely over the 5-gallon bucket and that, when equipped with the toilet seat, looks quite attractive. I also use sawdust as a cover material, and instead of putting the waste into the outhouse, I deposit it onto a thermophilic (heat generating) compost pile where, after several years, it turns into totally organic material. I would like to claim title to this idea but sadly, I can't. I read it in the aptly titled *Humanure Handbook* by Joseph Jenkins—an invaluable, entertaining, enlightening, and extremely well-researched read. You should see how beautiful my flower garden is.

Overall, living the cabin life is a pretty swell way to exist in Alaska. On your way to the outhouse at night you might even get treated to the northern lights—something those with indoor plumbing just can't appreciate. For daily aurora forecasts, visit the UAF Geophysical Institute's website at *www.gedds. alaska.edu/AuroraForecast.*

CARHARTT, FLANNEL, AND DUCT TAPE EVENTS

If you're all dressed up in your Carhartts with no place to go, or just got a new roll of duct tape that you're dying to use, keep these festivities in mind.

Duct Tape Ball
Where: Anchorage
When: February
What: Dress up in your best homemade duct tape duds and raise money for charity at this annual "only in Alaska" ball. Drinks, dinner, and dancing.
Information: 907-646-8600, *info@anchorage.net*, *www.anchorage.net*

Classy Carhartt Ball and Travel Treasures Auction
Where: Anchorage
When: March
What: Compete for Classiest Carhartt look and participate in an auction fundraiser. Sponsored by the Alaska Travel Industry Association.
Information: 907-929-2842, *atia@alaskatia.org*, *www.alaskatia.org*

Crusty Carhartts Contest, Carhartts Relay Race, Carhartt Fashion Show
Where: Alaska State Fair, Palmer
When: Last week of August, first week of September
What: Model your grossest Carhartts, create an original piece of fashion using some item of Carhartt clothing.
Information: 907-745-4827, *info@alaskastatefair.org*, *www.alaskastatefair.org*

Carhartt and Flannel Ball
Where: Fairbanks
When: October
What: Music, dancing, food, silent auction, prize for best-looking Carhartts—good times.
Information: 907-457-8453, *webmaster@akborealforest.org*, *www.akborealforest.org*

Carhartt Ball
Where: Talkeetna
When: December

What: Contestants tell stories about their Carhartts and how they saved their lives.

Information: 907-733-2330, *www.talkeetnachamber.org*

COFFEE: THE OTHER ADDICTION

It's no accident that in every Alaskan city with more than six residents there are espresso stands on every corner. The coffee business up here is simultaneously lucrative, highly addictive, and thriving. We Alaskans could feed small nations with the amount of money we spend on our coffee habits. Last I checked, I had four different "coffee club" cards in my wallet from different establishments around town.

Sometimes, with all the mind-numbing cold, the lack of fashion accessories, and giant predators at large, it gets hard to focus on normal, everyday life here in Alaska. But I've found solace with coffee. It's calming in a "gotta have it" jittery sort of way. I got this nifty little espresso maker for my stovetop so I can make coffee drinks any time I want in the comfort of my own home. Then on the way to town I stop at Java Joe's to see what's on special and grab a muffin.

And that brings me to another observation. The coffee addiction doesn't stop at coffee. The coffee Bigs know that you're bored with the bagels that have been served with coffee since time immemorial. So they ply you with live music in a comfy coffeehouse atmosphere in which fresh-baked smells waft through the air. You'll have a hard time resisting spending at least ten bucks in their establishment on a daily basis, and pretty soon you've got punch cards for a cookie club, a muffin club, and a sandwich club—by the time you dig through your wallet for the right card you're pretty thirsty. So you'll order an iced coffee. Geez, it's genius.

I need to buy a coffee house.

Of course, once you get a taste for good coffee, it's hard to settle for just any old coffee. Truck-stop coffee almost makes you gag. Instant coffee should be designated for space missions. You reserve regular grocery store coffee that comes in cans for your fallout shelter. That's when you realize that you're a coffee snob. On your next trip to Seattle you plan for three days of coffee tastings. You start saving money to travel to Ethiopia so you can tour coffee plantations.

Stayed Too Long

After looking in the mirror one day, David A. James decided to write this letter.

You know you've been in Fairbanks too long if:

Your seasonal affective disorder set in on June 22. You think God's a Republican. You're pretty thrilled about the arrival of Wal-Mart. After nineteen years you're halfway finished with your two-year master's degree at University of Alaska–Fairbanks. You think that Thai food is indigenous to Alaska.

You protest abortion when it's 40 below. You protest President Bush when it's 40 below. You're a Bible Baptist. You're a Unitarian.

You think the Soviet Union still exists, citing public schools, libraries, and emission testing as proof. You leave your pickup running for the entire month of January. You keep more guns in your house than the army has at Fort Wainwright. You still vote Alaska Independent Party.

Your front yard looks like it was transplanted from rural Tennessee. You shoot any squirrel that comes within 50 feet of your dwelling, just in case it's headed for your insulation. You prefer blue foam to porcelain. You wear your darkest clothing while riding your mountain bike without lights through the ice fog when it's 40 below.

You spend all your income on beer and dog food. You consider the crowd at Ivory Jack's (local bar) your family. You haven't had a girlfriend since 1986. You showed up for a seasonal job and stayed.

You're shocked to learn that some people in America don't own Carhartts. You didn't know that tarps came in any colors other than blue. You've heard persistent rumors about something called indoor plumbing. You celebrate July Fourth as the first day of fall.

You've heard folks on talk radio discussing these critters called Democrats, but seeing as you've never encountered any for yourself you call up Fish and Game and ask if they grow 'em here in Alaska and, if so, can a fellah bag one in a same-day land-and-shoot.

You're fairly certain that North Pole is zoned for meth labs. You get the *Northstar Weekly* for the articles. You write letters to the *News-Miner.*

Don't blame seasonal affective disorder, it's just who you are.

Reprinted with the permission of David A. James.

You give tax-free donations to free-trade coffee companies. You hang up a picture of Juan Valdez in your bedroom.

Even with all this, you're better off than when you were suffering needlessly in a dark cabin with a gun to your head. So really, a coffee addiction isn't so bad. And you could be spending your money on worse things—like Krispy Kreme donuts. Hopefully, that chain never makes its way this far north. Until then, run, don't walk to the nearest coffee stand and get yourself a mocha. Make that a double. It's never too late to support an Alaskan tradition and start an addiction.

THE ALASKAN VEHICLE

The Alaskan vehicle is a many-headed Sasquatch. Usually big, sometimes curious, but mostly covered in dog hair. Just as in the rest of the country, many folks here have embraced the "bigger is better" culture of gas-guzzling SUVs and Hummers. But fortunately, you can still find those original, "only in Alaska" type of vehicles that make you look twice. There are enough independent thinkers still on the roads here, and their vehicles can be quite interesting. For one thing, we don't salt our roads, so there are many old or "classic" vehicles that have survived the test of time. And by "classic" I mean the owner has spray-painted the phone number of his business on the side. Another truck I see around says Joyota instead of Toyota, and it *is* a happy-looking, multi-colored, graffiti-painted truck if I do say so.

What you gotta have up here for your car is a dog. I've seen cats and even a couple parrots in cars, but dogs are by far more popular. Sometimes they even seem to be steering the vehicle with no apparent impedance to the driver. But most times their happy heads are sticking out an open window or they're pacing around the bed of a pickup waiting to attack any passing car as if it were a runaway wiener on wheels.

Winter in Alaska poses an entirely different set of challenges for cars. You're going to need a battery blanket, oil-pan heater, winter extension cords, and excellent, if not aggressive, driving skills in order to jockey into parking positions closest to electric plug-ins. All of this will ensure that your vehicle will actually start when you want it to—something that is completely taken for granted in warmer, sissier climates. And don't forget to wrap that long extension cord around the driver's side door mirror after every use. This is cool. Spare tires are also recommended for when your tires turn from circles to squares during really cold weather. You must also equip your Alaskan car with the necessary survival equipment in case of an emergency. This includes chocolate, toilet paper, and the classic Alaska book, *Coming Into the Country* by John McPhee. It's got 417 pages. You can burn it to keep warm.

The common denominator among cars in Alaska is a cracked windshield. Because the Department of Transportation coats our roads with rock and not rock salt in the winter, and most of our "highways" are dirt, you will sooner or later end up with a wrecked windshield—evermore lining the pockets of wealthy windshield repairmen. So, if you don't have a cracked windshield yet, by all means go out and drive around and get yourself one.

Many people will argue that the Subaru wagon should be declared Alaska's state vehicle. You would be hard pressed to travel more than 5 miles without seeing a Subaru in the mix. Who is driving these Subarus? Professors, students, intelligent types, moms with children and dogs, outdoorsy types, baristas, skiers, clowns, and people who need a reliable vehicle for cheap. That's just the short list. These cars seem to run forever. We finally retired one after it racked up 200,000 miles, and it was still running. You probably won't find snowmachine enthusiasts or hunter types driving Subarus. Neither will you find construction or mine workers driving this lesser vehicle. These rugged people prefer either old character trucks with a gun rack, tool box, lots of dents and dings, and perhaps a mismatched panel or two, or large, mostly brand-new pickups with good towing capacity. These folks like to haul boats, four-wheelers, snowmachines, dirt bikes, and the like with their

Symptoms of Alaska Residency

You know you're an Alaskan if:

- You measure distance in hours.
- Your income is highest in October.
- You know how to pronounce Knik, Valdez, and Tanana.
- Your fleece jacket has almost as much hair as your dog.
- You own moose nugget jewelry.
- You think Igloo coolers or cardboard boxes with a little duct tape make great luggage.
- You know how Chicken (the town) got its name.
- You're tan from the wrist down.
- You learned how to swim indoors.
- Your first vehicle was an ATV, a snowmachine, or a boat.
- You don't wear a coat if it's 20 degrees Fahrenheit or warmer.
- You know at least one pot grower.
- King crab legs are a Tuesday type of meal.
- Anything less than a 200-pound fish is small.
- You do all your shopping online.
- You don't call the cops when you hear gunshots.
- You will never join Greenpeace to save Alaska from willows or scrub alder.
- You spend $150 or more for pumpkins and Christmas trees.
- You check the heater first before you buy a car.
- You buy your groceries two months at a time.
- You refer to our biggest city as Los Anchorage.
- You're a fan of Hobo Jim.

- **You know small dogs make good eagle bait.**
- **There are people in Hawaii who know you by name.**
- **You could pick out the guy from the Alaska Airlines logo in a lineup.**
- **You have duct tape on at least one article of clothing.**

hearty rigs. Most will be extended or quad cabs. And don't be surprised if you find window stickers of some cartoon character peeing on something or a bumper sticker akin to "Guns don't kill people, people kill people." These kinds of trucks might also sport a stout moose guard as well as extra lights, and they seem to be popular with military folks too.

But a good portion of Alaskans also prefer older, rugged types of vehicles. These include old Land Rovers and Land Cruisers, Jeep Wagoneers, old Ford and Chevy trucks, VW vans, and standard Jeeps. Of course there are also lots of people who drive real pieces of art, literally. Like moose antlers mounted on the hood of a car or the vehicle outlined with Christmas lights. That's what I love about Alaska. You can get away with that here.

To complete the look of an Alaskan vehicle, you should get a roof rack for your car or a pipe rack for your truck. That way you can haul all your canoes, kayaks, skis, and other outdoor gear with ease. You can also run around with extra gas cans strapped to the top of your vehicle with bungee cords—a classic Last Frontier statement. Oh yeah, and if your license plates expire, don't worry about it. The cops will be too busy busting meth labs in North Pole and Wasilla to bother with you.

IF YOU WANT TO FIT IN, YOU'LL NEED THIS

You've arrived. You found a cabin, got a truck, and bought some Carhartts. You've almost got it all, except for one thing—someone to keep you warm at night. Someone to be your everlasting companion. You need someone who will love you unconditionally and will stick their head out of your car window just for the fun of it. That special someone who will wake you up with wet kisses and will never refuse a walk with you. That someone might not have the best breath, but you can't have everything.

You need a dog. You just can't live in Alaska without having a dog. You have to watch out though, or you'll end up with another and then another, and pretty soon you'll think about getting into mushing and you won't even know what hit you. It happens to a lot of people. Just another casualty of living here.

But before you get a dog, make sure you have the time and amenities for it. Winters are cold and any animal deserves to be treated right. There are plenty of shelters and rescue organizations out there that will help you select the perfect dog and you'll be saving a life at the same time. Unfortunately, lots of sled dogs end up at shelters in Alaska because they didn't make the cut on a dog team for one reason or another. They might make better skijoring dogs or are just getting too old to be competitive. Maybe they come from a litter that was too big. Some are just born couch potatoes.

A handful of mushers and skijorers take in sled dogs from the pound and give them a second chance through the Second Chance League out of Fairbanks. Individual sled dogs are placed in foster homes where their abilities for mushing or skijoring are determined and then enhanced through training. The dogs are also assessed to see whether or not they are good with kids, other pets, or if they have any medical limitations. The dogs then become available for adoption, where they are paired with an owner best suited for them.

So, go ahead and get yourself a dog—any dog. Just remember to check the pound and the rescue organizations first. Then roll down your window and let your dog get happy. After that you can worry about getting your wood cut.

Here are some shelter and rescue organizations to check out online for more information about adopting a pet in Alaska:

- MuttCats.com (*www.muttcats.com,* click on "Shelter Directory" then "Alaska")

- AnimalNet for Pets (*www.shelters.theanimalnet.com,* click on "Alaska")

- Second Chance League (*http://members.petfinder.org/~AK17/index.php*)

From One Cheechako To Another

New York native Doug Fine came to Alaska in search of a life connected to the earth but instead found a steep learning curve and chain saws with teeth as sharp as a grizzly's. Learning how to survive and adjust to life in rural

Alaska, Doug describes his ascent from cheechako to well-adjusted Alaskan with humor and panache in his well-received book, *Not Really an Alaskan Mountain Man*. Visit Doug's website for more about his adventures (*www. dougfine.com*).

Q: In your book, you talk about growing up in suburban New York and lacking the ability of "Knowing How to Do Things." These things included "killing one's own food and starting a fire with wet wood." When you moved north to Alaska, you say you wanted "contentedness in a life of tangibility." That and "Knowing How to Do Things." So how did all that work out for you?

A: Well, I'm miles ahead of where I would be if I'd stayed in the suburbs. You can't Know How to Do everything. But for whatever reason, I felt happiest, most together, most in touch with the realest me, when I was at least *trying* to do some of the basic things all humans did before the mechanical and corporate ages came about. As *Not Really an Alaskan Mountain Man* makes clear, I am not very *good* at those essentials, but just trying allows me to sleep well, allows me to know myself better and to feel inspired often.

One other point on this: it took me a *long* time to see improvement in basic skills like, say, building. A year after moving to Alaska, I was still barely able to be an assistant drywaller at a friend's house. Since then I've erected an outhouse that has stood up to winds so far, and am planning a solar home. Likewise, I failed miserably at hunting in *Not Really an Alaskan Mountain Man*. Now I can catch my winter's worth of fish. But my progress has been remedial, to say the least. Meanwhile, in the course of all this happiness-pursuing, I tend to have so many cuts and splinters and abrasions all over my body that my dad apologizes to his apartment doorman for my appearance when I visit the folks in New York.

Q: In an effort to become a Mountain Man, you needed to learn how to use a chain saw so that you could cut wood for the winter and not die. Can you tell us about that experience?

A: First off, I find wood chopping—the manual step once the tree is in rounds—to be one of the more satisfying tasks in cold-climate life, mainly because it requires so little skill. You're outside, puffin' steam, looking at the earth around you, and satisfyingly hacking at hunks of it. With almost no brain power and just a little momentum, satisfying Stacks of Results pile up next to you—and they mean you won't freeze to death. On the chain-sawing step, yeesh, the memory of my early travails still fill me with dread. Because I should be dead. I guess my suggestion would be always wear eye and ear protection, sharpen the chain frequently, and consider electric chain saws (charged by solar or wind) since they're less polluting.

Q: If you had to choose the five most essential things a person would need to live in Alaska, aside from heat, food, and shelter, what would they be?

A: Ah, this is the question I was waiting to answer. Nothing like choosing a geographic location to be incompetent in, and suddenly five years later being a source of advice. So I'll shoot this out to other potential cheechakos who might also love the *idea* of being alive as a member of the animal kingdom, but who, like me, didn't have a lifetime preparing for the essential skills.

1 Exercise constant vigilance. In other words, expect the worst and plan accordingly: if someone tells you that a bad winter would mean chopping a massive pile of wood two stories high, chop one three stories high.

2 Visualize the needs of the next season (or seasons) months in advance. In other words, think and work one or two seasons ahead. It takes a couple of years at least to understand the seasonal cycles of a place and the associated survival requirements. For instance, in my part of Southeast Alaska, you gotta get the herring during their one-day run nearby in April, so you can use them as bait for the king salmon in May. Think of it this way and you're in good shape: it's always time to prepare for some task a couple of weeks or months down the line.

3 When in doubt, get outside, even on the yuckiest or coldest of days. Even for just twenty minutes. It'll almost always make for a more spectacular, exuberant day. On a related note, reducing the number of inputs in your life is one of the key benefits of rural living. Everything intensifies—you learn about yourself and what you really need just from building an outhouse or chopping wood.

4 In severe, genuine subarctic or arctic coastal rain (like when fishing), wear rubber-based rain gear. The expensive, space-age materials sold in outfitter stores *will* soak through.

5 Be careful about small-town gossip. In fact, avoid it. Since there are few televisions in rural life, we tend to become each other's soap operas. The gossip gene is stronger in some than others, it is rarely kind and rarely accurate. Everyone has been the target, and everyone has done it, but I early on made an effort not to let it become a major part of my life.

Q: **Describe a "day in the life" of the quintessential Alaskan.**

A: I've found rural Alaskan life to be energized to the point of busyness, especially during the long daylight time of year. Every day is really three days from May through August. As a writer, I might be up, have a run, eat breakfast, honk a few notes on my saxophone, and write half a chapter in a book before heading out to work as a river guide for six hours. After that, my circadian rhythm pumped and confused by the lack of "go to sleep—it's dark" commands, I might meet friends for a barbecue, check the crab pots, and head to the library to check my e-mail. The seasons so much determine the typical day. In the fall, of course, it's constant wood chopping. In the summer, it's fish processing. We're like squirrels, only we don't stash nuts. We can fish.

Blazing Ball of Eye Poison: The Bane and Blessing of the Midnight Sun

Some Alaskans put aluminum foil or heavy blankets over their windows to seek refuge from the deluge of summer sunlight. Others just don't sleep. We boat, we camp, we build. We fish and grill out a lot. We grow giant vegetables in our gardens and celebrate summer solstice with a mixture of jubilation and trepidation, as this midpoint of summer signals the inevitable turning toward winter again. But still, we enjoy our midnight golf, baseball, and costumed foot races. By the end of summer, most are tired of battling mosquitoes, ready for winter— ready to settle into a good book and get some sleep already.

TO SLEEP OR NOT TO SLEEP: STUPID QUESTION

Sleep. In Alaska it's a double-edged sword. In the summer, with the ever-loving sun shining twenty-four hours a day and an endless amount of Things to Do, sleep is the last thing on our minds. Especially when we've been stealing the so-called night away watching for Hairy Man (Alaska's version of Sasquatch), who's been robbing our gardens of giant blue-ribbon cabbages. Some say it's just the moose, but I'm among those who are not convinced. Hairy Man has to eat too.

Then in the winter, when it's only 6:30 p.m. and it's already been dark for three hours, we fight to keep ourselves out of bed until at least 7:00. Anything less than fourteen hours of sleep is a real bummer.

We resort to all kinds of ways of keeping the sun out of our bedrooms in the summer. The local grocery stores can't keep enough aluminum foil on the shelves. Heavy curtains, flags, and blankets also grace our windows. After a long day of fishing, gardening, hunting, gathering, building, boating, or working, some can fall fast asleep as soon as their head hits the pillow. Others resort to heavy sedatives and Barbra Streisand.

I remember one cabin I lived in had a window through which the sun shined directly on my face at about 11:30 every night as I lay in bed. One night I dug out my pink-tinted snow goggles and settled in for a nice, rose-colored sleep. Early in the morning I was awakened by a commotion out in the yard. I shooed a moose away from my garden and then figured since I was up, and it looked like rain, I would take my laundry down from the clothesline. With no laundry basket at hand, I decided just to wear the clothes as I took them down. So with about ten T-shirts, four pairs of jeans, socks on my hands, and a bra wrapped around my head, I made my way back to the porch. I leaned down a minute to quiet our dog, who was still barking at the moose, and when I stood up I was eye to ski-goggled eye with my husband, who was at the window in his underwear. He promptly let out a holler and did one of those quick moves a person might make when dodging a bullet. I guess the goggles spooked him. I was spooked too. I didn't think he still owned any tighty whities.

Sleeping in Alaska isn't easy, but I think your body will tell you when you need to sleep even if the sun still shines at midnight. Just don't give up on it. Work harder, play harder, or have a glass of wine before you go to bed. And get some decent underwear for goodness sake.

TOP 10 THINGS TO DO ON SOLSTICE

1 Watch a midnight baseball game without artificial lights.

2 Build a raft for the Homemade River Raft Race in Nome. Winners get to keep the trophy for a year—a fur-lined honey bucket.

3 Dress up in a crazy costume for the Midnight Sun Run in Fairbanks.

4 Gather a picnic and head up to Eagle Summit at mile 107 on the Steese Highway. From there you can watch the sun sink and then rise without dipping below the horizon.

SUMMER RECREATION

If you ever say you're bored in Alaska you should move to Iowa and see what you think of that. It's a great place to be a cow, but even the cows wish they lived in that flashy state with the Corn Palace—what is it, South Dakota? Here in the Far North there are myriad ways to keep yourself occupied in the summer, not the least of which is watching your back for toothy predators as you pick berries. Another summer favorite off the top of my head is fishing in the pouring rain. Odds are in your favor for that. And relatives. Alaska is a relative magnet.

Summer offers an endless array of recreation choices. In fact, too many choices, because you still have to do all the Regular Joe stuff necessary for living here. Like cutting wood for the winter (that dang season is always on our mind), fixing the roof, tending the garden, cutting the grass, building a shed, filling the freezers, etc. Oh yeah. And you gotta work.

So there sit the canoes, the ATV, the guns, the fishing poles, softball mitts, backpacks, the raft, your bike—all begging for attention. There's just not enough summer to go around. Some people devote themselves to just one sport, as in my friends' case—a drinking team with a softball problem. Others try to fill every weekend with any of the aforementioned activities and are rarely at home. Most of us wake up in the spring and dive right in, not coming up for air until October.

Then there are all of the celebrations and festivals that happen in the summer and I gotta tell you, we're ready for winter when it comes. But until then, you slap on that happy summer face and go out there and wear yourself out.

5 Stay up all "night."

6 Go camping and read a book in your tent at midnight.

7 Jump into the frigid water of the Bering Sea in Nome for the annual solstice polar bear swim. Full submersion will get you a certificate. (Yay!)

8 Throw horseshoes at a local watering hole and dance the "light" away.

9 Play a round of midnight golf.

10 Host a midnight fishing tournament with your friends.

SOLSTICE CELEBRATIONS

The farther north you go in Alaska the more daylight you get in the summer. Barrow, for instance, gets a full twenty-four hours of daylight on solstice (June 21), whereas Ketchikan gets just over seventeen hours. So solstice celebrations are more prevalent the farther north you go, but most towns celebrate this longest day of the year in some way or another.

The Fairbanks Midnight Sun Festival is probably the best solstice festival in Alaska, rolling in with just under twenty-one hours of daylight at the end of June. Food and craft vendors set up downtown, with local music from noon to midnight. There's also a Midnight Sun baseball game with no artificial lights, featuring the semipro Gold Panners team. This baseball tradition started in 1906 and is a festival favorite. Then there's the Yukon 800 boat race that runs from Fairbanks to Galena and back on the Chena, Tanana, and Yukon rivers. And over three thousand people show up every year for the 10k Midnight Sun Run that winds through Fairbanks' streets to the merriment of all the lawn-watchers who host BBQ parties to root for the runners, walkers, and wildly costumed competitors—which is, in my opinion, the best reason for participating in the race. I don't know too many places where you could run through the streets dressed as Wonder Woman and not draw stares. Last year I dressed up as a dumpster diver and my friend was the dumpster. I even had a fake raven flying over my head—and everyone was asking me why I didn't dress up. The first-place winner in the costume division was a porcupine. That guy ran 6 miles in a porcupine costume! He got the last laugh though—a plane ticket to Hawaii. They gave me soap on a rope.

BEST SUMMER FESTIVALS AND FAIRS

Alaska is packed full of things to do, but don't miss the fun of summer's festivals and fairs.

Golden Days
Where: Fairbanks
When: July
What: Festival honoring Fairbanks's gold-speckled past, complete with Rubber Ducky Race, grand parade, old-timey games, comedy night, street fair, car show, beer and wine festival, and live music.
Information: 907-452-1105, *info@fairbankschamber.org*, *www.fairbankschamber.org*

Girdwood Forest Fair
Where: Girdwood
When: Around the Fourth of July weekend
What: "No dogs, no politicians, no religious orders, no beer outside the beer garden." The annual rules for this festival have been in effect for thirtysome years but haven't hindered the good food, groovy tunes, happy hippies, arts and crafts, and games that are spread out in the trees in the lovely ski-resort town of Girdwood. Craft vendors can only sell handmade items and food vendors can

only sell noncarnival-style fare. Also expect a paragliding exhibition, parade, and 5k run too.
Information: 907-783-2931, *www.girdwoodforestfair.com*

Copper River Wild! Salmon Festival
Where: Cordova
When: Second weekend in July
What: Cordova's wild weekend includes five Alaska salmon fun runs along the scenic Copper River Highway, the Salmon Jam Music Festival, arts and crafts, a food fair, and the Prince William Sound community picnic.
Information: 907-424-7260, *visitcordova@ak.net, www.cordovachamber.com*

Moose Dropping Festival
Where: Talkeetna
When: Second weekend in July
What: Food, arts and crafts vendors, live music, parade, and softball tournament. There are also wacky contests like the "moose-dropping game," during which shellacked and numbered moose turds are dropped from a net onto a bull's-eye—closest and farthest nuggets from the bull's-eye wins. And check out the mountain mother contest, in which Alaskan mothers run through an obstacle course of outdoor skills.
Information: 907-733-2330, *www.talkeetnachamber.org*

Southeast Alaska State Fair
Where: Haines
When: Last week of July
What: Parade, food, live music, exhibits, most lovable dog contest, logging show, clown contest, fiddle contest, zucchini contest, softball, volleyball, disc golf, and horseshoes.
Information: 907-766-2476, *seakfair@aptalaska.net, www.seakfair.org*

Tanana Valley State Fair
Where: Fairbanks
When: Early August
What: Great Interior fair with rides, food, arts and crafts, vendors, animals, giant veggies, entertainment, exhibits, stupid pet tricks, Lego contest, old-time fair contests, talent show, and a pet look-alike contest.
Information: 907-452-3750, *fairinfo@tananavalleyfair.org, www.tananavalleyfair.org*

Alaska State Fair
Where: Palmer
When: End of August, beginning of September
What: Rides, food, exhibits, more giant veggies, vendors, animals, entertainment, flower gardens, crusty Carhartt contest, homesteader events, senior joke/storytelling contest, best Spam recipe contest, husband holler, and toddler trot.
Information: 907-745-4827, *info@alaskastatefair.org, www.alaskastatefair.org*

THE $24,999 FISHING HABIT

Fishing is a fairly straightforward thing. You put a worm on a hook, drop it in the water, and voila!—you can catch a fish. But no—men don't see it that way. In order to participate in this sport, men claim they need an assortment of fishing-related paraphernalia (boats, gear, beer). They are not above trickery or even faking a terminal illness in order to buy more toys to fulfill their last request. My friend Lori's husband is a prime example.

It all started with a toy boat that she put in his Christmas stocking. Soon after, he started taking baths with it and seeking out mud puddles. But when he started bringing it to bed, she had to draw the line. This just wasn't normal behavior for a grown man. She'd had it. She gave him permission to buy a real boat—a *small* real boat.

Soon enough, he announced that he'd bought a used kayak ($650). A kayak is a good place to start. "Honey," he said, "this kayak fishing is really great!" He was happy, for a while.

After a few months, though, he wanted a skiff ($2,500). A skiff is bigger and safer, he said. He could catch bigger fish with a skiff, he said. And he needed a trailer ($700). And a motor ($4,500). He begged. She buckled. Anyway, maybe she'd take the kayak. He seemed really happy. They ate more fish. She was happy, he was happy.

But then he did a little river fishing with his brother and caught more pike than he ever had in his whole life. Big ones. Saw a bear and a moose too. She could see this one coming.

Despite the kayak and the skiff, now he wanted a flat-bottomed river boat ($2,500).

"Fresh pike all the time, honey!" he exclaimed.

"Uh-huh," she groaned.

"Haven't you always wanted to try out that pickled pike recipe?"

"Oh yeah."

"I'll even take you for a riiiiiidddeee…"

Now they had three boats (total cost: $10,650). But, with the new boat, he wanted a new trolling motor (new total: $11,400).

Not two weeks later, his friend, a charter boat captain, offered him a day out on the water with him and some clients. It was a stirringly calm, blue-sky day. They limit out on halibut, red snapper, and even catch some silvers. There are hands on deck that clean the fish. No one gets sick. This thoroughly impresses Lori's man. It's a real manly man day. He comes home with a cooler full of fish and a cigar hanging out of the corner of his mouth. He's got some big plans. He looks her straight in the eye and says, "This is it, honey. I think we should get in on this."

She poured herself a drink and held it to her temple. "Get in on what?" she said with a smirk. She had to hear this.

"Well, just think of it—when your dad comes up next year, wouldn't it be nice to take him out in style?"

That was a low blow! How could she refuse something better for her own father? "I don't know, honey love," she said. "I think Daddy would be happy just to be here." She swirled the ice cubes in her glass and waited for his reply.

"Really?" he said, undeterred. "Huh. I didn't figure you like that."

He'd never taken that angle before. She was confused. There was silence while they each plotted and schemed.

"Listen, I'll sell my other boats," he said. "A buddy at work has got a nice 24-footer for sale right now ($24,999) and selling the others would cover about half of that cost. You can even sleep in it! We could go anchor in some quiet little cove for the weekend, and you could take the kayak, and we could throw out some lines and boy—doesn't that just sound great? Just you and me?"

"And my dad," she added.

"Of course, your dad too. I'll put the boats in the paper tomorrow."

"What about the kayak?" she reminded him.

"It's as good as sold!" he barked triumphantly.

"No, I thought it was mine?" she said.

"Oh yeah. Yes, it is yours, honey. It's yours. We won't sell that."

"*You* won't sell that."

"Right."

Ten days later her man had successfully unloaded his skiff and his river boat and was the proud owner of a new oceangoing vessel with sleeping capacity (curled up) and cool lights and stuff. The fish on her table now cost upwards of $25,000 with interest. No wonder she brags about them.

Fishing Tournaments

Winter King Salmon Tournament
Where: Homer
When: March, one day only
Entry fee: $100
Prizes: Over $90,000 in cash and prizes. Keith Kline from Kenai won the cash prize in 2005 with a 35.32-pound king and pocketed $21,819.
Information: 907-235-7740, *viscenter@homeralaska.org, www.homeralaska.org*

Homer Jackpot Halibut Derby
The Largest and Longest Running Jackpot Derby in Alaska
Where: Homer
When: May 1–September 30
Entry fee: $10 derby ticket
How to win big: Catch the biggest halibut of the season.
Prizes: Tagged fish cash prizes, random cash drawing from all ticket stubs of the season, weekly top-fish cash prizes, kids cash prizes. The big winner in 2005 took home over $48,000 for a 310-pound halibut.
Information: 907-235-7740, *linda@homerhalibutderby.com, www.homerhalibutderby.com*

Valdez Halibut Derby
Where: Valdez
When: May 20–September 3
Entry fee: $10 daily ticket or $50 season ticket
Prizes: First place, $15,000; second place, $5,000; third place, $2,000; plus a drawing from all derby tickets for a new truck.
Information: 907-255-4727, *info@valdezfishderbies.com, www.valdezfishderbies.com*

Sitka Salmon Derby
Where: Sitka
When: Last weekend of May, first weekend of June

Entry fee: $30 ticket
Prizes: Cash and merchandise
Information: Sitka Sportsmen's Association, P.O. Box 3030, Sitka, AK 99835, 907-747-6790

Seward Silver Salmon Derby
Where: Seward
When: Third and fourth weeks of August
Entry fee: $11 daily ticket, or $52 for entire derby
Prizes: $10,000 for biggest fish, more cash prizes through tenth place. Other cash prizes for tagged fish, daily heaviest fish, and special categories.
Information: 907-224-8051, *visitseward@seward.net, www.sewardak.org*

Valdez Silver Salmon Derby
Where: Valdez
When: July 9–September 3
Entry fee: $10 daily ticket, or $50 season ticket
Prizes: First place, $15,000; second place, $5,000; third place, $2,000; plus merchandise prizes throughout the derby.
Information: 907-255-4727, *info@valdezfishderbies.com, www.valdezfishderbies.com*

MOSQUITOES AND THE MOSQUITO MAGNET REVOLUTION

I'm surprised there aren't more deaths in Alaska from mosquito-induced blood loss. Mosquitoes are probably the main reason Alaskans move to Lower 48 cities. Those rotten little buggers can't get a foothold amongst all that city pavement, which makes for pretty darn attractive living. That and the closer proximity to espresso stands must lure those Alaskans away.

But times they are a changin'.

There is now a machine available called the Mosquito Magnet to remedy the situation. This machine is designed to simulate a living, breathing human, which is all but certain to trigger the battle cry of the little suckers, thereby attracting billions of them directly to your door. Yes, you pay money for this. Of course these machines don't look human though. That would be spooky (although a true human look-alike might be a good marketing angle for crime-addled suburban areas). No, these rural units look much like a portable grill with either electric or propane hook-up and they emit CO_2, heat, and moisture, enticing said mosquitoes with these remarkable human characteristics. The machine then traps the unsuspecting mosquito when she comes for a look-see (only female mosquitoes bite). The human reward comes in emptying a suicide bag full of dead mosquitoes and the satisfaction of knowing that you may have saved your family a trip to the hardware store for guns with which to kill themselves.

There are some things you can do to naturally reduce your exposure to mosquitoes. Willem Takken and his colleagues at Wageningen Agricultural University in the Netherlands found one species of mosquito that is attracted to stinky feet and Limburger cheese. Dark clothing also initially attracts mosquitoes from a distance, and sweat is a certain lure because of the chemicals it contains. Floral or fruity fragrances should be avoided, as well as swamp camping.

One out of ten people are highly attractive to mosquitoes, confirming the theory that one person may be bitten more frequently than the guy next to him. Breathing is also something that calls in hordes of mosquitoes—especially vigorous breathing. Unfortunately, the only remedy for that will cause death.

DEET, the old standby for repelling mosquitoes, is still the preferred and most effective means for keeping them away. It should not be applied to skin, though, as I've seen the stuff all but eat through clothing. Put enough of it directly on your skin and I suppose you could just up and disappear. Citronella candles are pleasant, but will only be helpful if you are sitting very close to them and then may set you on fire.

In Alaska, everyone uses Pic's mosquito coils. These coils of suspicious, yet effective material burn like incense, giving off a heady smoke that will last for hours. This stuff really seems to work, and although you don't necessarily want to breathe it in, it will repel mosquitoes.

The age-old scenario of human swatting mosquito will play out in yards and wilderness areas all over Alaska for generations to come. That, ultimately, cannot be avoided. Don't lose sleep over the 175 known species of mosquitoes that will fly over 40 miles for a meal though. You can either stay locked in your house forever—or get a bug zapper. That's what I'm going to do. Those things are cool.

GIANT VEGETABLES

Large, face-rearranging bears have nothing on Alaska's reputation for giant cabbages. Nope. Ask any Alaskan whether they'd rather grow a giant cabbage or get attacked by a bear and they'll pick the giant cabbage every time.

I don't know what it is. It's crazy—almost an obsession for some. Maybe we just get bored with all the normal Alaskan things that go on. You know—staying warm and dry and not crazy. Then one day someone says, "Hey, check out this giant cabbage that I grew." And son of a gun if it ain't the best thing you've seen since indoor plumbing. But trying to get at the details of how it's done is another thing entirely. Some say it's a trade secret. Others call it a "family recipe." My family's got a recipe for pickled eggs that I wouldn't give to just anyone, so I can sort of understand. I came across the gravestone of a once-prominent blue-ribbon cabbage grower and it read, "I'm still not telling."

The kind people at the Alaska Cooperative Extension Service say it's supposed to have something to do with all of our sunlight, rich soil, and cool temperatures. I don't think my permafrost-rich soil is what they're referring to, but I can grow the cutest little frozen cabbages you've ever seen. I don't think anyone else is doing that.

Other publications hint at things a grower might do to increase a cabbage's size, like planting it in a tire filled with soil. This is supposed to either keep the plant warmer or make it easier to roll into the judging ring at the fair. I guess these things really like fertilizer to grow big, so one book said that it wouldn't be a bad idea to plant your cabbage directly on a compost pile. I'm not desperate enough to plant any cabbage in my outhouse, but the idea is curious…Then there's the issue of water. They say cabbages like a steady supply of water. This is a real bummer for those without a well (me). Other than that, they say in order to duplicate the California growing climate, you'd have to move there. Yeah, right.

The state record for a cabbage is held by Barb Everingham of Wasilla. Her green giant weighed in at 105.6 pounds at the Alaska State Fair in 2000. Curiously, all of the biggest cabbages on record have been grown in Wasilla—kind of an Area 51 for cabbages it seems. But another fellow living in Palmer is giving everyone a run for their money in the category of insanely large, yet inedible vegetables. (The real big stuff doesn't taste that great—grainy and tough.) Scott Robb currently holds five world records for the following:

- 75.75-pound rutabaga in 1999
- 42.4-pound kale plant in 2001
- 63.3-pound celery that stood 5 feet tall, in 2003
- 39.2-pound turnip in 2004
- 64.8-pound cantaloupe in 2004

This self-described "psycho grower" has, unlike other regular growers, given up some of his secrets of success. He uses water on his plants that's been warmed to 80 degrees Fahrenheit, feeds them a "secret blend" of rabbit and chicken manure through irrigation tubes, vacuums the leaves for pests, and installed an underground air-conditioning system to keep his cold-loving cabbages at the ideal growing temperature. Sounds easy enough. In 2005 his cabbage claimed second place at the fair. The next thing he wants to outsize is the watermelon. I'd personally like to see him work on Kit Kat bars.

If none of the above inspires you to plant a garden, consider this: the biggest cabbage at the Alaska State Fair takes home a $2,000 check. Second place gets $1,000, and third $500. Holy cruciferous vegetables! That's enough to convince me. Now I've just got to figure out how I'm going to tell my husband that I just ordered a dump-truck load of chicken manure and that the drillers will be here tomorrow to start on the well.

Resources for Gardening in Alaska

Alaska Cooperative Extension Service (*www.uaf.edu/ces*)
An excellent source of information about gardening in Alaska, with publications you can download or order for free.

Explore North (*www.explorenorth.com/ag-ak.html*)
Good information about agriculture and gardening in Alaska.

The Alaska Gardener's Handbook, **by Lenore Hedla**

Alaska Gardening Guide, **by Ann D. Roberts**

Alaska's Farms and Gardens, **by the Alaska Geographic Society**

FIRE-BUILDING PRIMER

If you're going to live in Alaska, you better know how to start a fire. And that includes starting fires in woodstoves, in the wilderness, in a fireplace, or under a freshly skinned can of SpaghettiO's. Everybody has their own way of starting a fire, but it's helpful to remember that if you get really desperate, you can use diesel fuel. Diesel can help you get a fire started, whereas gasoline can blow you up. Yet gasoline might be helpful if you live in the Southeast, because nothing in that rainforest is going to burn. So I need to remind you—be very careful in the Southeast because if you get lost there, you're going to die. On that same subject, there's no wood in the Arctic, so avoid that area too. No sense in sugar-coating it, it's life or death out there.

HINTS FOR FIRE STARTING

- Start with dry materials smaller than a pencil.

- Don't start your fire until you have gathered enough wood to keep it going.

- If it's winter or raining and you can't find any dry wood, locate a standing dead tree and chop it down or chop pieces out of it to get a fire started.

First, you should have some nice, dry wood. Of course you'll never have dry wood on hand in real life so here are some suggestions for fire-starting materials to keep handy. Individually wrapped alcohol swabs from a first-aid kit, or better yet, an alcohol pad wrapped around a cotton ball, make excellent fire starters. Small candles and lint from a clothes dryer are also good. But birch bark is by far the best fire starter and will burn even when wet. Use this with small tinder materials and you'll be sure to make Prometheus proud.

Next, before you ignite your initial materials, gather sequentially bigger pieces of fuel to feed your fire until it can stand alone. It is common knowledge that if you leave your juvenile fire alone while you go off for more wood, it will be gone when you get back. Happens all the time. Those teenage fires can't be trusted. So gather enough wood to keep it going, and don't take your eyes off it.

Now comes the fun part—lighting it, which should only take one match. Unless that match craps out and you have to use a second. But a real sportsman will only admit to using one match. Yes, that fire has the potential of keeping you alive but it doesn't "count" if it took more than one match to start it. It will, on the other hand, "count" if you die, so diligence is encouraged.

Then, there's also the 9-volt-battery-touching-steel-wool way of starting a fire. That's kind of fun. Just remember that it does produce fire if you try it for kicks at the dining room table. If you really want to be challenged, try starting a fire with a bow drill. This method uses the friction of wood against wood to start a fire, and primitive peoples are said to have used this method for centuries. But seeing how they're not around anymore, you be the judge of whether it worked out for them. If you're feeling lucky though, give it a try.

That about wraps it up. Not only will fire keep you warm, it will boost your mental status in an emergency situation, can be used as a signal, and is a necessary Alaskan skill. Just remember, one match good—two matches bad.

For more information on starting a fire with a bow saw or about survival in general, check out *Tom Brown's Field Guide to Wilderness Survival*. Your head will spin.

THE FINE ART OF GRILLING

If any kind of natural disaster were to threaten Alaska, I think people would grab their guns first, then their dogs, then their BBQ grills. By the looks of the grills on every porch, deck, boat, and tailgate (the kind that's rusting in the yard, not the kind you take to a football game), you'd think that Alaskans don't own any indoor cooking appliances at all. Except for hot plates—those things are great.

This phenomenon might result from a strong showing of the "grilling stock" in this state. This is a stock of men who have been bred over the centuries with adaptations for cooking food over an open flame. Or in the modern sense, over an 8-foot-long $700 stainless steel Sam's Club gas grill with a small refrigerator, counter, and sink attached. "Uuff uuff." They haven't determined how to breed the "drinking while grilling gene" out of men yet, so the refrigerator is really handy for keeping beverages cold. The sink, on the other hand, never gets used. A woman obviously designed that grill.

There is something to be said for the aroma of a good cut of meat sizzling on the grill. I always know when my neighbors are grilling. I don't think anything carries on the wind like good old-fashioned charred meat.

I guess grilling just gets under your skin. Literally. The charred areas of any grilled substance are supposed to be carcinogenic. Like that's going to stop us. We've got freezers full of fish, moose, and caribou and it's not going to cook itself. Besides, eating is one happy way to die.

There's also the argument concerning gas versus charcoal grills. To me, it doesn't really matter. I think charcoal grills impart a better taste to the meat and put out a better smell into the wind when cooking (good for calling in rogue bears to kill you). But they take a long time to get warmed up, so if you're really hungry, you'll chew off your right arm before you ever get any meat cooked (that, or start eyeing your pet reindeer). Gas grills heat up instantly and cook food just as fast. There's always the threat of running out of propane, but a prudent griller is always prepared with some kindling. And that's another source of fire and flavoring. Grilling over an open fire or with wood in a charcoal grill really gives food a nice flavoring. Nice, gritty, ash-covered flavoring. Besides, I've always said that the smell of a campfire is my favorite perfume. Impart a cooked food smell on that and I'm a man magnet.

OK. So go out there with all this inspiration and get grilling already. And if you're looking for a date, or a present for your date, get a grill and you'll be armed and dangerous.

FIRE STARTERS

- Cotton balls
- Alcohol pads/swabs
- Lint from clothes dryer
- Candles
- 9-volt battery and steel wool
- Magnesium stick
- Birch bark
- Small stick shaved like a porcupine
- Dirty underwear

5

Hot Tubs, Christmas Lights, and Cable TV: Good Winter Living for the Cabin-Fever Bound

There are many ways to survive an Alaskan winter, one of which is flying off to some beach and forgetting the whole thing. For those that stick around though, winter can be overcome with just a few necessities, like cable TV, flashing Christmas lights, and a hot tub. There's lots of other stuff to do, but only these three count. Read on for some time-tested advice on how to make it through the winter without killing yourself.

TRAPPED BY THE HOT TUB

Winter in Alaska is almost better than summer in Alaska. The tourists are gone, the mosquitoes are gone, all that ugly green foliage is gone, and that ever-lovin' sun is gone. We Alaskans are one happy group of people to hang out with. A little messed up come February, but by and by, decent. The only things that keep us sane are hot tubs. That and chocolate. Booze is good too. But you have to be careful. Those hot tubs can be dangerous.

My husband and I gained a healthy respect for hot tubs the winter we were stranded in the Aleutians posing as caretakers (think back to Chapter 2, which described this fantasy island winter). We could only reach the nearest village by taking our 18-foot skiff across a 3-mile stretch of water, but because this particular body of water just happened to be the Bering Sea with Bermuda Triangle–like currents and tides, and our only protection should we fall in were our life jackets (ha, ha), we didn't go to "town" much.

Aside from the treacherous death run to the village, it was a peaceful and stress-free existence. Except for the mean homestead dog and the daily thrashing by 80-mile an hour winds. And the bears—don't forget about those! Then there was the not-so-trivial matter of gathering driftwood to keep the place warm and that a person can only eat so much beans and rice before they start to act a little funny, and damn if ptarmigan don't make impossible targets!

So there might have been a little stress. But nothing that a little booze and the hot tub wouldn't fix. Yes, down there on the beach, in the snow, looking over the gray ocean, that glorious, wood-fired hot tub. Hot water. Smoke. A crackling fire. Stars. That wooden hot tub was the only reason to exist in that godforsaken place.

Using it, though, required some effort.

One particular afternoon seemed especially good for a soak, so I bundled up and headed down the narrow footpath that led to the beach. I gathered some kindling from the shed and within a few minutes had a small blaze going in the submerged stove that would heat the water in the tub. I rubbed my blue fingers over the orange flame and eyed the cold ocean water in front of me. Jumping back and forth from foot to foot I giggled and thought about how good it was going to feel.

I ran back up to the homestead and glanced at the clock. In 45 minutes, I would repeat the process all over again.

Usually the water was good and hot by the time the fourth full load had burned down to coals. But this is where things got tricky. You see, depending on the level of patience and/or desperation of the individual initiating the hot tub ritual, said water might seem practically "boiling!" after a mere three firings.

"Come on honey," I said to my husband. "It's ready."

"It's ready already?" he replied.

"Yeah, it was pretty warm last time. Come on."

He followed me down the path to the shed where we would strip naked. This in itself was always a tense moment. Naked at 15 degrees Fahrenheit with the Aleutian wind swirling around your...well, around your body parts. Let's just say it's not like a day at the warm naked beach. We tip-toed hurriedly through the snow to the tub and Dave jumped in first.

"I don't know about this," he said. "It's kinda cold."

"Can't be! Is it?" I plunged my hand in and didn't think it felt that cold. I jumped in too.

"Ahhhhhhh...Ohh. It's freezing!" I yelled.

We stood up, our bodies cold and rigid, and gazed up the hill to where the house stood warm and glowing in the fading daylight. A gust of arctic wind rushed across our shoulders.

"No way," I howled, plunging myself back into the tepid water. A slow, luke-warm death sounded better than a quick, icicle-up-the-footpath kind of death. In an instant, Dave followed suit.

"Remind me to never let you be in charge of this whole hot-tub thing again," he growled. "We're trapped."

Our only hope was the fire in the stove, still burning strong. If it could warm the water just enough to ward off the looming hypothermia, we would make it. As long as there was smoke coming out of that stack, there was hope. But there would be other challenges.

"I have to pee," I said.

"Well go do it," Dave dared, motioning his hand to the outhouse just a few feet away.

The thought of that made me have to pee even more. I didn't move.

An hour passed. There was less and less smoke coming out of the stack. The water had warmed some, but it was not yet comfortable, let alone hot.

By this time, we had managed to pull the plywood cover back over the tub, leaving just enough room for our heads to stick out. We were getting hungry. We watched low-flying seagulls skim our heads and wondered how they would taste. But unless they landed there on the edge of the tub, we would never know. Not even a flying meal was going to lure us from the relative warmth of our tomblike existence.

We had now been in the tub for an hour and a half. There was all but a thin wisp of smoke coming out of the stack. Dave was just as cold as I was, but he knew that I wasn't going anywhere. He finally pushed back the cover and took a long, deep breath. I've never seen him move so fast. He ran to the shed, grabbed some wood, and was stoking the fire before I even noticed he was gone.

"Is it cold out there?" I asked coyly.

"I'm going to kill you!" he screamed, shivering, and then did an uncanny Dukes of Hazzard move over the side of the tub and dunked me under.

In another half an hour, the water had warmed and we had successfully averted a gruesome welcome for the homestead owners come spring. As soon as we could, we got the heck out of there and headed back to the house no worse for wear. Except for an extreme case of wrinkled skin. Next we got out the booze.

When You've Got Cabin Fever

- Host a talent show—you can only pantomime to KISS songs.

- Contact an old enemy.

- Eat a stick of butter.

- Dress up in theme, say, like a cowboy or a surfer or a chicken.

- Go shopping with counterfeit money.

- Play strip poker (not with old people).

- Try standing on your head.

- Taste-test world vinegars.

- Create a family collage using pictures from a wrestling magazine.

- Draw what you think you'll look like when you're eighty.

- Talk in rhymes.

- Instead of walking, skip everywhere.

- Tie a jingle bell to your cat's tail.

- Leave prank messages on friends' answering machines.

- See how much chocolate you can eat in a day.

- Write down ten things you're going to do if you ever get false teeth.

- Try to break-dance.

- See how many french fries your mouth can hold.

- Tell everyone they have to do a cartwheel before dinner.

- Photocopy your face at the office. Hang it on your fridge.

- Advertise your friend's car for sale on the local radio program—real cheap. Give his number.

- **Build a house with a stack of cards after five cups of coffee.**
- **Learn the phrase "You are so stupid!" in a different language**
- **Start an arm-wrestling tournament at work.**
- **Ride your toddler's tricycle around the kitchen.**

THE $5,000 TV HABIT

If you want to be popular in Alaska this winter, get the biggest TV you can't afford, subscribe to the most inclusive satellite package offered out of California, and then put a bag of chips on your overturned Igloo coffee table. Now turn the weather down to 30 below and in an instant you'll be transformed from the geek of the week to the soup de jour.

But before you go getting a big head about your charming, albeit technologically advanced, financially strapped self, I have to say—it's not about you. It's about your 52-inch flat-screen HD plasma TV with 965 channels. It's about your Bose surround-the-cabin sound. It's about the little twinkly lights in your TV room, the Coleman fold-up movie theater seats, and your popcorn machine. It's about that giant homing beacon of a satellite dish on your cabin roof that is calling in all the two-channel losers to your place so they can hook up their IVs to your TV. You may live in a one TV-room cabin, but brother—you got it goin' on.

The only reason these kinds of people work at all is so that they can support their TV habit. Their credit cards are maxed out, but in an odd twist of fate they keep seeing commercials on TV advertising bigger and better television technology and get suckered in. Next thing you know they're at Sam's Club looking to buy a TV the size of a Ford pickup and giving their old, VW Rabbit–sized TV to the needy.

It's a darn harsh reality out there with all that snow and cold and people that live in your house. The warm glow of a TV set can replace all but the most annoying family interactions, making a darkened winter a real blessing for some. For others the lure of the TV is interrupted only in the event of a chimney fire or a beer run.

So indulge yourself. Go get that giant TV, cozy up with your soon to be ex-whoever, and settle in for a long, happy winter. Turn on that homing beacon and you'll have all the friends you could ever want. All you need now is one of those red glowing EXIT signs above your door to make your Alaska home theater experience complete. I think those are pretty cheap.

A SEASONAL GUIDE TO FIREWORKS AND HOLIDAY LIGHTS

Don't let anyone fool you—Alaskan winters are harsh. Before considering illegal activities, try some good ol' fashioned holiday lights to brighten your mood. Here are some tips to help you get started.

September

Put out all of your holiday lights now. If you wait any longer, you run the risk of putting them up in subzero temperatures, and those flimsy little wires will snap like a frozen Charleston Chew. This also proves to be a legitimate reason for leaving them up year-round, as opposed to the reason so-called rednecks leave them up. I don't know that reason, but I realize it's a fine line that we walk.

Halloween

Get some big lighted pumpkins, because real pumpkins will just freeze and their faces will contort. Orange lights are nice too. You also need one of those motion-sensor activated dummies that looks fake but at the same time real enough to be quite freaky when its mouth moves and it says something. Kids love that.

Thanksgiving

Giant lighted turkeys and little pilgrim people will let the world know that although you live in Alaska, you are indeed aware that the United States of America celebrates this eating holiday and are thankful that you can buy poultry within 100 miles of your current location. A glowing cornucopia on your roof will really set off the mood.

Christmas

It's time to pull out all the stops and keep up with the Joneses, who have obviously been shopping at the new Wal-Mart. Really light things up. If you can't see the northern lights anymore because of the glow in your yard, you're halfway there.

New Year's Eve

Go to Alabama and get some illegal fireworks from one of those roadside stands where someone in a gorilla suit nearly assaults you as you exit your vehicle. New Year's is our Fourth of July. You're not really trying unless you spend at least as much on fireworks as on the year's wood supply.

January

There are no holidays, save for Martin Luther King Jr. Day, and anything that includes the reverend in any kind of lighted display might be both tacky and hard to come by. Keep the Christmas lights up.

Valentine's Day

Red, pink, and white lights are easy to find and will delight your mate when he comes home to see the big glowing heart in the window and the giant blow-up Snoopy Valentine shining under floodlights in the yard. When you discover he got you a new multitool to express his love, the Snoopy figure will make a great target. It's February. Somebody has to die.

St. Patrick's Day

By now the sun has returned in force, so no lights are needed. And after all, this is a drinking holiday—it's the tradition we've been waiting all winter to justify. No need to distract with green lights.

FEEDING THE BIRDS OF WINTER

Winter is a great time for getting up close and personal with the birds that inhabit Alaska's bleak season. According to the Alaska Department of Fish and Game, over twenty-five species of birds stick around for the harsh winters of Interior and western Alaska, while over a hundred species remain in the milder, coastal areas of the state. So while winter bird feeding may not come with summer's species variety, an intimate look into the lives of these small creatures can brighten even the darkest winter day.

COMMON WINTER BIRDS IN ALASKA

Black-billed magpie

Black-capped chickadee

Bohemian waxwing

Boreal chickadee

Chestnut-backed chickadee

Common raven

Common redpoll

Dark-eyed junco

Downy woodpecker

Gray jay

Gray-crowned rosy finch

Hairy woodpecker

Hoary redpoll

Pine grosbeak

Pine siskin

Red-breasted nuthatch

Rock dove

Steller's jay

Three-toed woodpecker

White-crowned sparrow

White-winged crossbill

First off, if you're going to set up a bird feeder, make sure you place it out of reach of bears or moose, which could become a problem if they interpret this tasty treat as an invitation for dinner. Next, you want to consider the location of your feeder. Birds naturally prefer areas with some shelter and protection from predators. If you don't have any vegetation in your yard, you could try to pile up some brush, or put out your Christmas tree next to the feeder when you take it down after the holidays.

To begin, start feeding the birds in the fall, when natural food supplies begin to diminish. As soon as one bird finds your feeder, more will soon come, and you should anticipate feeding the birds all winter long until natural food supplies again become abundant in the spring, as they will come to depend on this food source.

There are many food choices for your feeder. The best overall food choice, in my opinion, is black oiled sunflower seeds. They tend to be eaten by the widest variety of birds at the feeder or on the ground. I wouldn't bother with wild birdseed mixtures, as they contain a high volume of filler seeds that are not eaten by most birds.

Thistle seeds tend to be favorites of redpolls, so I have a feeder of that just for them. Other seed-eating birds such as sparrows, pine siskins, grosbeaks, and crossbills will also enjoy thistle, as well as crushed raw peanuts, wild grains, and scratch feed.

Chickadees and woodpeckers enjoy suet, so I like to have a few suet cakes or homemade suet balls available for them.

Magpies, gray jays, Steller's jays, and ravens will eat just about anything you put out for them. I often throw out stale bread for their enjoyment. Avoid moldy bread, though, as this can make them sick. Fruit and other table scraps will be eaten too. These bigger birds can be quite hoggish, but they add a real fun twist to the bird-feeding regimen.

I like to scatter seed on the ground or on a piece of plywood for birds like juncos and grosbeaks that don't like to feed at the feeder.

All in all, for just a few dollars for seed, feeding birds is a great winter pastime. Feeders are easy to build too and can provide a nice winter project. You can keep a birding book next to the window and every time you see a new bird, you can check that one off your list. Before you know it, you'll find yourself reaching for that book in the summer too, as your interest in birding blossoms and the great bird migrations fill the Alaskan sky.

Resources for Alaska Birding

Alaska Bird Observatory (*www.alaskabird.org*)
Maintains the observatory for education, research, and information purposes.

Alaska Department of Fish and Game, Division of Wildlife Conservation (*www.wildlife.alaska.gov*)
Click on "All About Wildlife" and then "All About Birds." The site contains lots of information about birds and other types of wildlife.

Birds in Alaska (*www.birdsinalaska.org*)
Low-key site with interesting links. Includes photos and field hints for bird watching in Interior Alaska by Jim Gilbert.

***Birders Guide to Alaska*, by George C. West**
Contains detailed information about finding Alaska's birds.

***Guide to the Birds of Alaska*, by Robert H. Armstrong**
The only comprehensive guide for all of Alaska's 443 bird species; includes photos.

THE NENANA ICE CLASSIC

If you're the type that likes to roll the dice, then you ought to place your wager on the most famous betting game in Alaska's history: the Nenana Ice Classic. Your $2.50 guess of date and time will be recorded along with thousands of other Alaskans who want to guess when the Nenana River ice will break up.

The contest started in 1917 with some Alaska Railroad workers placing bets on when the ice would go out. Since then the guessing game has turned into a statewide phenomenon that has doled out over $10 million in prize money.

The village of Nenana, located 75 miles north of Denali, plants a tripod in the Nenana River every year, with a trip wire attached to an official clock. When the river begins to break up and the tripod moves enough to trip the clock, the winning time is recorded and the winners are announced. A weekend festival kicks off the event and includes contests and family entertainment.

Visit the official home page of the Nenana Ice Classic (*www.nenanaak iceclassic.com*). To learn more about the village of Nenana, visit the community's website (*www.nenanahomepage.com*).

WORLD ICE ART CHAMPIONSHIPS

Every year Alaskans are treated to an international phenomenon that brings together skilled artists from around the world to behold the clearest ice on earth. For two amazing weeks, master ice sculptors chisel away at huge blocks of ice, transforming them into works of art in the world's premier ice-carving event: the World Ice Art Championships in Fairbanks. The amount of talent and skill that goes into each piece is amazing, considering that the medium is just a chunk of ice.

But not just any old ice. The ice harvested for the competition—some 1,500 tons each year—is said to be some of the clearest in the world. "Arctic Diamonds" it's come to be called. The ice is extracted from gravel ponds that have no current running through them, so no bubbles form while the ice freezes. And with Fairbanks temperatures averaging what they do (cold, colder, and somebody shoot me!), the ice grows mighty thick. The ice is so clear you can read headlines from a newspaper through a 40-inch polished block.

The competition is divided into two main classes: single-block and multi-block. For the single-block competition, teams of two are given a 5 x 8 x 3-foot block of ice weighing approximately 3,000 pounds and have sixty hours to complete their sculpture. The multiblock competition gives four-person teams twelve blocks of ice measuring 4 x 4 x 3 feet and weighing in at 7,800 pounds each, for a total of 36,000 pounds, or almost 18 tons of ice! The multiblock has a time limit of 110 hours. The classes are then divided into the categories of "realistic" or "abstract."

Great Alaskan Books for Winter Reading

Here's a short list of some of my favorite Alaskan books to help scratch that cabin fever itch:

- *Alaska Wilderness: Exploring the Central Brooks Range,* by Robert Marshall
- *Arctic Daughter: A Wilderness Journey,* by Jean Aspen
- *Arctic Homestead,* by Norma Cobb and Charles W. Sasser
- *As Far As You Can Go Without a Passport,* by Tom Bodett
- *The Last Light Breaking: Living among Alaska's Inupiat Eskimos,* by Nick Jans
- *On the Edge of Nowhere,* by James Huntington and Lawrence Elliott
- *One Man's Wilderness,* by Sam Keith and Richard Proenneke
- *Ordinary Wolves,* by Seth Kantner
- *Trapline Twins,* by Julie and Miki Collins
- *Two in the Far North,* by Margaret E. Murie and Terry Tempest William
- *Two Old Women,* by Velma Wallis

Many different tools are used in creating the sculptures. Chain saws, chisels, dentist drills, and Dremel tools are the most common, although some sculptors improvise their own tools. Pieces are mortared together using slush, and hair dryers are used to smooth the ice when needed. Many artists work round the clock and will continue working right up until the last seconds of the competition. Some sculptures will end up nearly 25 feet tall and use almost every bit of ice.

When the judging is finished, the ice art is illuminated with colorful lights to highlight each one at night. The pieces are judged on artistic and technical merit.

The Ice Park is located strategically among spruce trees so that the sculptures are shaded from the sun. The event also features a kids' area with cool ice slides, twirly tops that you can sit in and spin, and all sorts of interactive animal and figurine sculptures to keep the little people busy. The kids' park defies age though, and many adults get in on the fun.

Amazing that these artists put all that work into these pieces of art only to see them melt soon after. It's akin to creating a beautiful painting and hanging it on the wall only to know that a fire will destroy your house the next day. The melting of ice sculptures is, though, a harbinger of spring, so I guess we have to take the bad with the good.

Go to Fairbanks to check out this amazing winter attraction. All that ice and those colored lights will really amaze you and take your mind off those long winter nights. A run down the slide won't hurt either.

For more information, go to the World Ice Art Championships website (*www. icealaska.com*). Fairbanks's website also has great information about ice art and other winter activities (*www.fairbanks-alaska.com*, click on "Winter Events").

To view ice sculptures in the summer, check out the Ice Museum in downtown Fairbanks—"The Coolest Show in Town" (907-451-8222, *www.ice museum.com*). This museum houses an 8,000-cubic-foot walk-in display case that maintains a temperature of 20 degrees Fahrenheit and showcases over 40,000 pounds of ice art. Also watch a multiscreen presentation of the ice art process from start to finish.

PREPARING YOUR VEHICLE FOR WINTER

One of the biggest challenges about living through an Alaskan winter is keeping your car running. There are several things you need to do to prepare your vehicle for the long cold winters.

Before Winter

- Check your belts and hoses.
- Check all fluid levels—power steering, coolant, brake fluid, transmission fluid—or have a mechanic check them for you at your next oil change.
- Top off your windshield-washer fluid.
- Inspect your windshield wipers for wear and replace if necessary.
- Make sure all lights in your electrical system are functional.

- Switch over to lighter, winter oil.

- Make sure your battery connections are good and clean. Many times a vehicle won't start because of this one issue.

You Will Need

- A battery blanket and a block heater. These two items are necessary for Interior winters especially. They essentially act like an electric blanket and give your vehicle a bit of warming before you actually start it. Without these two items, you may never make it out of the driveway.

- A winter-rated extension cord. This type of cord is designed to withstand colder temperatures. Regular extension cords are stiff and may break in frigid temperatures. Buy one for home and one for your trunk so you can plug in your car at work or the store if needed.

- Good snow tires. Studded tires are good, as are many winter-rated wheels. Just don't venture out with bald tires or you may not live to see another winter.

In Case of an Emergency

The items on this list can be stored in a large duffle-type bag in your trunk or wherever you can find room. This is especially important if you will be going on a long drive in an area with limited services (e.g., anywhere in Alaska).

Heavy blanket or sleeping bag	Parka, mitts, hat, boots
Flares	Jumper cables
Flashlight or headlamp	Candy bars
Candles	Tow rope
Bag of sand or cat litter	Chemical hand warmers
Matches	Small shovel
Cell phone	

Starting a Vehicle without Plug-ins

If you live in an area without electricity or are going to recreate in such an area and will be leaving your vehicle for a few days, you will need to have a means to start your car when you return. Here are some ideas:

- Invest in a weed burner (a long-handled torch that attaches to a propane tank) and a couple sections of stovepipe (one straight, one elbow). Light your weed burner and direct the heat through the stovepipe, which you should position (carefully) under your oil pan. Drape a tarp or a blanket over the entire front of the vehicle to aid in warming.

- Bring along some charcoal and lighter fluid and a large roasting pan or cookie sheet. Fill the roasting pan and light. When the coals are hot, place under your car and cover the front of your vehicle with a tarp or blanket to aid warming.

- Bring along a large metal coffee can and use in the same fashion, with charcoal or wood coals. This is also good for starting snow machines, except you must dig a hole in the snow and place the snow machine over the top of the heat source.

- You can bring a generator along if you've got one, but it may not start in the cold either.

Of course with any of these suggestions, the idea is to not set your vehicle on fire, so use good judgment. In any case, bring some kindling, a hatchet, and an armload of wood with you so you can start a warming fire while you wait for your car to heat up.

WINTER FESTIVALS

Talkeetna Winterfest
When: December
What: Bachelor Auction, Carhartt Ball, Wilderness Woman contest, tree lighting, and parade of lights.
Information: 907-733-2330, *www.talkeetnachamber.org*

Homer Winter Carnival
When: Early February
What: Parade, school carnival, Spamtacular Spam-off (Spam art), fireworks, homebrew contest, flea market and craft show, Homesteader's Social, Kachemak Nordic Ski Club's Wine and Cheese Tour, and Beluga Lake Lodge Mardi Gras Kings Ball.
Information: 907-235-7740, *www.homeralaska.org*

Ice Worm Festival
Where: Cordova
When: February
What: Parade, blessing of the fleet, ping-pong tournament, variety show, Ice Worm Queen coronation, food fair, arts and crafts, survival suit races in harbor, longest edible ice worm on display, photo show, and fireworks.
Information: 907-424-7260, *iceworm@ctcak.net*, *www.iceworm.org*

Alyeska Winterfest
Where: Alyeska Resort, Girdwood
When: February
What: Ski demos and clinics, mountain bike slalom, tubing, snowshoe race, ice skating, paragliding exhibition, polar bear plunge, and fireworks.
Information: 907-754-2108, *guestservices@alyeskaresort.com*, *www.alyeskaresort.com*

6

Dumpster Diving, Bike Riding, and Other Thrifty Ways of Exciting Living

Just the other day while admiring the parka I had on, a woman asked me if I had made it myself. When I told her I got it at the dump and that the beautiful white ruff on the hood came from an old antique coat she said, "Now that's my kind of shopping." I am not ashamed to say that I get a lot of good stuff at the transfer station—you know, the place where we take our trash. These places offer thrilling possibilities for finding valuable treasures. Many cabins are built and furnished with "dump finds." Other bargain sources range from garage sales to radio classifieds. Nowhere else but Alaska could you find a wolf pelt and an exercise bike for sale side by side. And if you are thrifty by necessity, not by nature, you are in good company here in Alaska, where people ride bikes year-round and live aboard their boats.

THE DUMP GIVETH, THE DUMP TAKETH AWAY

I get most of my outdoor gear from the dump. Heck, I get clothes, windows, rugs, and even jewelry there too. Gold jewelry. No kidding. They call them "transfer stations" up here. It's just a big parking lot edged with dumpsters where we bring our trash, because we don't have pickup this far north. Guess it hasn't caught on yet. The dump proper is actually in a different location. Anyway, in one corner of the parking lot is a covered platform—a place to recycle things, if you will. Got a new fridge but are too lazy to put the old one in the paper? Take it to the platform. Garage sale leftovers? Take it to the platform. Old doors or flower pots? Yes, leave them at the platform and someone will happily take them home.

You know the feeling you get when you find a $20 bill on the ground? That same feeling is potentially available each and every time you go to the dump. What will you find today? What do you need? Inevitably, what you need you will find, and what you find, you better pick up—at least until you decide if you *really* want it. If you don't, the person looking over your shoulder will pick it up to decide if *they* really want it, and so it goes, on and on. There is no time for second-guessing. This is true especially if new goods are being unloaded from someone's vehicle onto the platform. The prudent "recycler" will offer to help unload the goods; this gives first-right privileges to dig through the stuff—at least the box you're hanging onto. Until you have abandoned that box, it is common knowledge that there is no pressure to "hurry" before someone else "gets it." Unlike the moments when two cars pull up at the same time to a pile of yet-untouched goods and sitting on top is, say, a very nice stereo. In that instance, the running shoes you picked up at the platform a few days prior will come in handy.

~~~~~~~~~~~~~~~~~~

MY 5 BEST DUMP FINDS:

1 **.22 rifle**

2 **Fur coat**

3 **Antique bed frame**

4 **Small diamond/gold ring**

5 **Jade and ivory carved Native figurine**

~~~~~~~~~~~~~~~~~~

There is no shame in all of this. And making rounds of the dumpsters is also acceptable and sometimes lucrative. I can't deny that I actually climb into them occasionally for something I want. The people there who share in this fun are usually very normal, friendly folk. Oftentimes I will strike up a conversation and it will invariably revolve around the last best thing either of us found or how many miles our Subarus have on them. Then we may lend each other a helpful hand loading something in (or on) our vehicles.

I used to drool over items in the Cabela's catalog, with all that fancy gear and all those expensive name brands. I used to think that I would never truly *know* the experience of fishing until I had a G. Loomis fly rod, or that if I only had those $500 "trekking" boots I would surely "trek" farther. (Poor people "hike." Those that shop at Cabela's "trek.") That was before I took the wool off my eyes and my "highly in demand" bachelor's degree in outdoor/adventure recreation management landed me a job bagging groceries.

I've learned that when it comes to buying good stuff, you're just rolling the crap dice. That expensive gear is either going to get smashed in the car door, stolen, or destroyed by your new puppy (or kids).

But then I overheard an interesting conversation about this guy finding a tent at the dump. He said it was missing a pole for the rain fly and had one small rip, but otherwise it was good. Nothing that a little duct tape wouldn't fix. This intrigued me. The next time I went to town I drove by the transfer station and noticed a flurry of activity. There seemed to be more people browsing than dumping, so I pulled in. That's when I saw it—an old Coleman stove, my first dump find! Turns out it needed a small fitting to work, but I felt good knowing I was doing my part to reduce the size of the landfill. The dump giveth, the dump taketh away. I was hooked.

I've since discovered that most cabins up here have some aspect of the dump built within, or are built with materials that are bartered, scavenged, self-manufactured, or found—which makes for interesting "curb appeal." We furnished our entire first cabin from things I found at the dump—*and* built the outhouse. The same goes for fashion. My parka came from the dump, as did the sheared beaver on my mittens from an antique coat. Shoes, pants, kids clothes, and even underwear (be picky, your choice) can all be found at the dump. Sometimes the local thrift stores drop off their "overstock." I've seen boxes and boxes of clothes left for the taking. I've even picked up some things and then sold them on eBay. How cool is that? The dump is really a great place to shop. Just get there early—the crowds can be ugly.

Insider Tips for Successful Dumpster Diving

Anytime is a good time for a visit to the dump, but weekend evenings seem to be particularly fruitful. People clean out on the weekends and the place really fills up. You will find more things in the summer than in the winter, but stop anyway because you just never know. And stay out of the way of the dump trucks. They just want to do their job without worrying about running over you, so give them plenty of room. The dumpsters can be just as lucrative for finding stuff as the platform. Don't be "too good" to make the rounds. Some folks use a "picker" to sort through things. Just find an old broom or mop handle, cut off the end, and add a nail.

Bonus tips:

- The ravens that haunt the dumps are truly fascinating. Take time to enjoy them. But don't leave groceries in the back of your truck while you're looking around the platform. Ravens are, after all, opportunists.

- The dump is a great place to find boxes for moving or mailing things.

- Pick things up for friends and relatives, or sell stuff on eBay. Donate to charities.
- Take your kids. There are lots of toys and clothes. Teach them the value of a dollar.

GARAGE SALES

If I don't find what I need at the dump, the next best thing is a garage sale. The nice thing about garage sales is that people moving away from Alaska don't want to haul all their stuff back to the states. This makes for good, cheap finds on everything from boats to books. You might even get more than you bargained for—a coffee-table book my friend bought was full of marijuana leaves. Yikes! Outdoor gear is also plentiful at Alaskan garage sales, so this is a good time to buy that new tent you had in mind. Just like exercise equipment, outdoor gear is often purchased with good intentions but is never used.

My advice for garage sales is to get there early. Show up 15 minutes before any sale opens. Even this is sometimes too late. Although, if the ad in the paper says "early birds will be shot," disregard this advice. The competition can be fierce—especially in the spring—people just go nuts for a good sale. You wouldn't believe how eager some folks are after a long, dark winter. The sale might be wiped out after the first 10 minutes. One last thing—always, *always*, barter on the prices. Don't be shy—just do it. And leave your dog in the truck while you shop. It might break something or eat the owner's cat.

THE BEST ALASKAN THRIFT STORES

I don't know too many people who don't like the deals they find at thrift stores. Sometimes it's hard to find things at other stores up here, and the thrift stores may be your only hope. And if you really want to fit in in Alaska, you don't want to look like you stepped out of a Cabela's catalog. For the look that says "I've been here a while," visit a thrift store and buy some worn-in Carhartts and a wool shirt. But stay away from anything that says "Alaska" on it. You'll look like a tourist for sure. Though, if it's, say, a work coat with a logo for an Alaskan business or a fishing vessel, you're OK.

Top 10 Reasons Why Cabela's Scratched Your Name from Their Mailing List

If you find yourself more and more at the dump and less and less poring over fancy catalogs, you may as well admit it. You've been sucked into the vortex that is the dump. It's all downhill from there.

1 Your last paycheck should just about cover dog food and a newspaper.

2 You catch yourself watching reruns of *Lifestyles of the Rich and Famous* while drinking Pabst Blue Ribbon in your sweats.

3 People who drive new Subarus are really starting to bug you. "Fancy pants!"

4 You overheard someone talk of scoring a real nice pair of boots at the dump and you can't help but feel cheated.

5 You pitch your tent in the yard and discover some pretty serious rips. Duct tape seems like the logical solution.

6 Gas prices are topping $3.50, but you still drive 10 miles out of your way to see if there's anything good at the dump.

7 Garage sales, you proclaim, are "too rich for my blood."

8 You tried to buy your last fishing rod on "senior discount day." You're twenty-nine.

9 Your yellow VW Rabbit seems too flashy. You start looking for a Chevy LUV pickup. Baby blue.

10 You invite your date to go to the dump with you. Four hands are better than two.

Most communities in Alaska have some type of second-hand or thrift store. Just ask around and the locals will point you in the right direction.

Fairbanks Rescue Mission Thrift Store (Too Good to be Threw)

This store is packed but full of incredible deals if you have the time to find them. Check it out. *1401 Cushman Street, Fairbanks, 907-374-8850.*

St. Vincent de Paul Thrift Store

Another great place to find a good deal. Lots of items and very inexpensive. *8617 Teal Street, Juneau, 907-789-5124.*

Salvation Army Thrift Stores

These stores are located throughout Alaska and carry clothes, household items, furniture, books, shoes, and more. The prices are better than Value Village (see below) but can be quirky—like a $30 price tag on a record player, or $10 for some old shoes. Still, the money you spend helps to support the Salvation Army's programs. Visit their website to find the eighteen store locations throughout Alaska (*www1.salvationarmy.org/usw/www_usw_alaska.nsf*).

Value Village

Value Village stocks the largest selection of items in their three Alaska store locations. Clothes are arranged by size and gender, and the stock changes frequently. You will also find household goods, furniture, toys, shoes, books, and almost anything else you might be looking for. Prices can sometimes be high, but for the most part you can still find good deals on quality items. *Anchorage: 5437 E Northern Lights Boulevard, 907-337-2184, and 501 E Diamond Boulevard, 907-522-9090; Fairbanks: 3027 Airport Way, 907-474-4828.*

The White Elephant

The ultimate thrift store experience! This awesome thrift store is not only a great place to find a good deal, but is a good place to rub elbows with the locals—literally. There are usually around twenty people waiting for this tiny, item-packed shop to open, and the rush that follows when the doors finally open is akin to a stampede. Items here are dirt cheap and the adventure can't be beat. *323 Seward Street, Sitka, 907-747-3430.*

RADIO CLASSIFIED PROGRAMS

The following radio stations provide some type of a classifieds program. This is a free (usually) call-in forum for listeners to buy, sell, or trade items in their area. This service is invaluable, especially if you don't have a Wal-Mart or Home Depot in your backyard. It's like going to a garage sale in the comfort of your own living room, and the callers can be downright entertaining.

ANCHORAGE

KBYR 700 AM
Tradio—buy, sell, trade
Saturday, 12:00 p.m.–2:00 p.m.
907-274-5299, 866-610-5297
myopinion@kbyr.com
www.kbyr.com

FAIRBANKS

KFAR 660 AM
Tradio—buy, sell, trade
Monday–Friday,
12:00 p.m.–1:00 p.m.
907-458-8255, 907-451-5999 (fax)
kfar@nmbradio.com
www.kfar660.com

GALENA

KIYU 910 AM
Yukon Wireless—announcements, messages, classifieds; also heard in Kaltag, Nulato, Koyukuk, Huslia, Hughes, and Ruby

Monday–Friday, 7:20 a.m., 11:45 a.m., 6:30 p.m.; Saturday, 8:00 a.m., 12:00 p.m.; Sunday, 12:30 p.m.
907-656-1488, 907-656-1734 (fax)
raven@kiyu.com
www.kiyu.com

HAINES

KHNS 102.3 FM
Radio Marketplace—buy, sell, trade
Saturday, 10:00 a.m.–11:00 a.m.
907-766-2020 (from Haines),
907-983-2853 (from Skagway)
khns@khns.org
www.khns.org

JUNEAU

KINY 800 AM
Problem Corner—buy, sell, trade
Monday–Friday,
11:05 a.m.–12:00 p.m.
907-586-1800, 907-586-3266 (fax)
kiny@ptialaska.net
www.kinyradio.com/problem.html

Kenai

KSRM 920 AM
Tradio—buy, sell, trade; classifieds
read on air and posted on web site;
$10 for one day, $15 for three days,
$30 for six days, or free if you call in
during the show and read it yourself
Monday–Saturday,
11:07 a.m.–12:00 p.m.
907-283-5811, 888-872-5776
rken18@radiokenai.com
www.ksrm.com

Kodiak

KVOK 560 AM
Hotline—buy, sell, trade, community
talk; $20 for a 7 day ad read on air
Monday–Friday, 10:00 a.m.–11:00 a.m.;
Saturday, 10:30 a.m.–12:00 p.m.
907-486-6011, 800-560-5865,
907-486-3044 (fax)
kvok@ak.net
www.kvok.com/hotline.htm

Kotzebue

KOTZ 89.9 FM/720 AM
Swap and Shop
Monday–Friday, 2:06 p.m.
907-422-3434, 907-442-2292 (fax)
kotz@otz.net
www.kotz.org

Sitka

**KIFW 1230 AM; simulcast on
KSBZ 103.1 FM**
Problem Corner—swap, sell, discuss
local issues
Monday–Saturday,
11:10 a.m.–12:00 p.m.
907-747-6626
kifw@gci.net
www.kifw.com

Valdez

**KCHU 770 AM; in Cordova on
88.1 FM; in Whittier on 88.3 FM**
Buy, swap, sell; not a call-in forum;
DJ reads classifieds on air for up to
two weeks
Monday–Friday,
12:06 p.m.–12:11 p.m.
800-478-5080
kchu@alaska.net
www.kchu.org

LAST FRONTIER BIKE RIDERS: A TOUGH BREED

It takes guts to ride a bike year-round. In a Fairbanks winter, you have to be just about crazy. Besides that, though, there are great benefits to riding a bike instead of driving a car—especially if you can't afford even an ancient Subaru. I recently chatted with one die-hard Fairbanks bike rider, Willis Fireball, a hearty ten-year resident, famed local singer/songwriter, and non–car owner.

Willis has an impressive history of long-distance bike trips under his belt, including a 4,400-mile trip from Fairbanks to Albuquerque in 1995 and a 600-mile loop on the south island of New Zealand in 2000. That's some serious leg power—and these trips only scratch the surface. Visit Willis's website to read about some of his travel adventures and sample his music (*www.willisfireball.com*).

Q: **First of all, why don't you have a car?**

A: It was originally a combination of cheapness and fitness that kept me from getting a car, and those two factors are still a huge driving force for me. But in the last fifteen years, I've grown to appreciate more and more my independence from gasoline. The economic and health benefits continue to reinforce my distaste for the convenience culture of automobiles. Before I went to college, I never thought of commuting as an opportunity to exercise. Like a lot of people, I'd often drive—sometimes quite a long way—to someplace so I could go running, biking, hiking, or whatever. My perspective has completely shifted.

Q: **What do you do for a living, and how far from work do you live?**

A: I am still a student. I work at the university. It's a very easy 2 miles from my cabin. For a while I lived a long 6 miles away, and in the winter that was a long commute. On the very rare 40-below days, I had to dress very carefully and the trip was indeed an expedition. I loved it, but it was serious business.

Q: **Does your bike have any special adaptations for winter riding? Do you have a seat warmer?**

A: No seat warmer. There are a lot of good winter biking adaptations, but lately I haven't been using any of them. For the past two winters I've been riding a poorly maintained touring bike. It's not even a mountain bike, which is pretty ridiculous.

Q: **Would any old bike do for general transportation? Could a person pick one up from say, the dump, and make it work?**

A: In general, in most places, in summer—yes, any old bike is fine. Better bikes will be easier and faster, but any bike can be made to work. This becomes a lot less so in winter, but as I said before, even in a Fairbanks winter a crappy bike will do.

Q: **How do you get groceries?**

A: I can carry a huge amount on my bike in panniers, a backpack, and my bike trailer. Usually, though, I take smaller loads and shop more frequently. A week of groceries goes easily in my bike panniers.

Q: **Any advice for those that want to, or have to, use a bike for transportation?**

A: You do what you have to. You'll figure out what clothes you need—and hopefully, without frostbite or injury, how to keep the bike working and how to ride better. The best equipment available at sports stores is good, but not necessary.

For excellent tips and advice on winter biking, visit the Fairbanks Cycle Club's website (*www.fairbankscycleclub.org*). For more winter biking inspiration, visit the Alaska All Season Cycling website (*http://home.gci.net/~winterbiker*).

LIVE-ABOARDS, ALASKA STYLE

It's not uncommon to find a small percentage of people living aboard their boats in most of Alaska's harbors. In Sitka and Homer around 10 percent of the boat slips are occupied by live-aboards. Living on a boat not only solves the problem of finding housing in places where there aren't many choices, but it is, by and large, a whole lot more economical as well—even though slip fees vary by harbor and additional live-aboard fees usually apply. At most harbors, basic amenities are available, like phone, electricity, showers, and the like. And some boats are even set up with cable TV.

Alan Horoschak is the vice commodore of the Baranov Yacht Club in Sitka and a part-time wildlife tour operator. He and his wife Liz have lived aboard their sailboat in Sitka since they brought it up from Hawaii in 1989. Alan and Liz are currently planning to buy a small English steel sailboat to tour the canals of Europe.

Q: Tell me about your boat and what kind of amenities it has.

A: *Jubilo* is a gaff-rigged schooner, 40 feet on deck and 55 overall, launched in 1920. We bought it in 1988 in Hawaii after it sank. My wife and I overhauled it with a new diesel genset [generator set], SS water tanks, RO [reverse osmosis] system, hot water cockpit shower, enclosed head, Dickinson oil stove, etc.

Q: How hard is it to get a permanent slip?

A: Just a matter of waiting in Sitka. *Jubilo* took four years.

Q: What's the most challenging thing about boat living?

A: As a couple, it is keeping the wife happy. Guys generally don't expect much in the way of creature comforts as long as it is fun and the beer holds out, but try to convince a wife that the head is a bucket used outside— especially in Alaska.

Q: Is living on a boat more cost-effective than living on terra firma?

A: Actually, if planned out, it is much more cost-effective, as you do not have the space for all the crap you collect living on the beach. Also, if one *has* to be out on the water, whether to fish, sail, or just to enjoy the outrageous scenery, then a good boat is the answer.

Q: What benefits does boat living offer?

A: Moving is easy, and if you don't like your neighbors, then...But really, I do not think people should live aboard unless they can think and do for themselves. Unlike a house, any boat can sink. It is a steep learning curve to follow to become competent, but in this day and age few things really are, and it gives a great sense of self-accomplishment.

Q: Any advice for Alaskans thinking of trying this type of living arrangement?

A: Don't try to go cheap, as everything on a boat is a trade off—it will either cost you time or money, and money is easier for most folks than the time to learn how to fix it.

7

Forget About Bears: How to Avoid a Moose Attack

Your chances of bumping into a bear in Alaska are possible, but most escape these unlikely encounters without incident. Moose, on the other hand...you can bump into a moose anywhere—on the road, in your backyard, in the city. And they don't seem dangerous. They seem as harmless and docile as a horse, leading you to believe there's nothing to worry about. But that's exactly why they're so dangerous. One minute they're happily munching on the fresh buds of your lilac tree, the next their ears are tucked back and they're coming straight at you. All the more reason to learn how to act around moose and what to do if you get attacked.

LET'S TALK ABOUT MOOSE

When you think of the North, probably one of the first images that comes to mind is moose. From Maine, to Canada, to Alaska, moose epitomize wild, northern country. Their ungainly stature, comically proportioned nose, and gigantic size make them memorable. Around 150,000 moose make Alaska their home, from Southeast Alaska to the Arctic Slope. Highly adaptable, moose are just as likely to frequent the backyard of an Anchorage home as the bank of a remote river. Moose and humans exist in a mostly harmonious relationship, with moose sightings generally enhancing the everyday Alaskan experience.

But when it comes to dangerous animals, we tend to dismiss the moose. Alaska is far more famous for its tales of grizzly bear attacks. We have been told over and over what to do if confronted with a bear attack and how to handle ourselves in bear country. But male adult moose (bulls) weigh in from 1,200 to 1,700 pounds and stand 6 to 7 feet tall at the shoulder. Cows (female moose) tip the scales at 800 to 1,200 pounds. Pester these critters or invade their space or come between them and their offspring, and you're prime real estate on the moose attack market.

It seems unlikely. Hardly an animal of nightmares, the moose of our youth was a cartoon character who hung out with a friendly squirrel sidekick named Rocky. It's hard to take moose seriously. People don't run for their lives when moose are nearby. They take pictures. They get closer. Maybe a little closer. Then they might get stomped.

Moose on the Loose

A few years ago, we had a young bull moose hanging out around our house for several weeks in late winter. We lived north of Fairbanks in a rural area with 6 acres of land and an empty valley behind us. The moose had discovered some straw that I had stashed under our shed and used as bedding for our dogs. One day as I came around the corner of our shed, I encountered the moose happily munching my straw on his knees just off the trail. I was surprised, but not too alarmed, so I approached within 10 yards of him and started to shoo him away. He was unfazed and stared at me, chewing. I yelled at him some more. "This guy is really tame," I thought. I stepped closer and flailed my arms some more. Then, like a light switch being turned on, he came at me—full speed ahead. I put myself in reverse as fast as I could and fell into the deep snow behind me. Luckily, it was a bluff charge, and the moose stepped off into the trees. I was stunned. At that moment I realized how I had seriously underestimated a moose's ability to attack. I was lucky I didn't get stomped.

That little bull wreaked havoc on my family for weeks. He became increasingly brazen and defiant of everything that stood in his path, making us look both ways before stepping away from the safety of our front door every time we went outside. We even fired bullets over his head with not much reaction. These kinds of moose are dangerous, but so is every wild moose out there. It's hard to remember sometimes that they are indeed wild.

Warning Signals and How to Avoid a Moose Attack

Moose are the biggest member of the deer family in North America. The *deer* family. Doesn't sound real threatening does it? But a 1,200-pound moose can exert deadly force with its legs by stomping and kicking if it wants to.

When moose feel threatened, they display common characteristics that are identifiable. If you see any of the following reactions in a moose, you need to give it some space:

- The moose looks right at you—has stopped feeding, eating, etc.
- The moose paces a little bit, licking its nose and mouth.
- The moose paws at the ground.
- The moose moves toward you.
- The moose's ears are laid back.
- The hair on the moose's neck and back is raised.

Sometimes, victims can be completely blindsided by a moose attack. In such cases, where the moose comes from "out of nowhere" at a full charge, the circumstance probably involves a cow protecting her calf, a moose that has been harassed or is stressed, or a moose that is in rut. Sometimes, dogs can provoke an attack—as far as the moose is concerned, a dog poses the same threat as a wolf. Moose may also attack if they are tired or hungry, as in deep-snow winters.

If a moose starts running toward you in a charge, turn tail and run. Try to get behind a tree or any other solid object. You can run around a tree a lot better than a moose can, so give it your all and don't stop until you're safe.

If you find yourself on the ground with an angry moose on top of you, curl up into a ball, cover your head as best you can, and don't move. The moose may kick, stomp, and paw at you with all the force of their weight coming down. They may even use their antlers. When the attack stops, be very careful getting up, as the moose may be nearby and provoked to attack again.

Keep the following in mind as you live and play in Alaska in the company of moose:

- Never feed a moose, no matter how tame or hungry he seems. This is illegal in Alaska.
- Never get between a cow and her calf.
- Give moose lots of space.
- Always keep your dogs under control.
- Never harass a moose.
- Never "fence" in a moose or block off its escape route.

- Know how to spot the signals of a stressed moose.
- Back away slowly and quietly if you encounter a moose at close quarters.
- If a moose is coming at you in a charge, run. Try to get behind a tree.
- If you see someone getting attacked, make loud noises to scare the moose—honk your horn, fire a gun, etc.

MOOSE ATTACKS

In Alaska, moose attack stories are like war stories: everybody has one. Due to the circumstances, some turn out more memorable than others. Here are three actual encounters with moose that bear witness to the danger and power of these animals.

Spruce Tree Saved His Life, Dogs No Help

Ken Cauffman of North Pole had just finished a day of fishing at his favorite stream near Paxson and would have never imagined that he would soon be running for his life. On his back was a pack full of camping gear and a limit of grayling and salmon. His two dogs were with him: Luke, a lovable shepherd-collie mix, and Yukon, a mischievous malamute. As the dogs were on the hillside investigating the smells of summer, Ken was alerted to something wrong. The dogs were yelping and snarling and the whole mess was coming toward him. Immediately, Ken drew his .44 pistol and readied himself for what he assumed was a bear. Yukon came into view first and flashed by Ken at full speed. Luke came next and upon seeing Ken, sat down half hidden behind a clump of dwarf birch, looking back with tongue hanging out.

Ken could hear something sizable crashing through the brush and was surprised at what appeared: a very large and agitated cow moose. "This animal wanted to kill something," he said.

Ken immediately turned tail and headed for cover behind a stunted spruce tree, the moose hot on his trail. "It was wild-eyed and looked 10 feet tall with ears laid back and neck hackles raised. It hissed and snorted and chased me around and around that little spruce," he recalled.

They made laps, this way and that, until Ken was nearly exhausted. At one point he shot off a round from his .44 to scare the moose, but with no effect.

The Great Moose Prank

Back in the '80s, a big draw for the Golden Bear Gift Shop in Tok was Bucky the Moose—a large taxidermied bull moose that stood outside the establishment under a small shed roof. Many tourists would stop to take pictures and even hop up on the saddled back of the long-dead moose to pose happily—like tourists do. I suspect many locals did the same.

After years of this fun, the owner decided that the aging, decomposing mount had to go. According to Gary Moore, who grew up in Tok, the owner took the moose to the dump and wiped his hands clean of it. But some mischievous locals had other plans. A few burly men rescued the discarded moose from the dumpster and deposited it outside of town, propped up in an opening visible from the road.

I should probably mention that this occurred in complete darkness the night before moose-hunting season opened.

The next morning, Gary's mom and aunt decided to do a little road hunting. It wasn't long before they came upon Bucky the Moose standing there in the opening. They jumped out of the vehicle with binoculars in hand and upon seeing horns, began blasting away, eventually emptying their rifles. The moose never budged. Upon discovering the prank, the women went directly to the troopers to complain.

According to Gary, Bucky the Moose was a sore subject around town for a while. Given the condition they found that stuffed moose in a few days later, it's no wonder the townsfolk were upset. In no certain hurry, the troopers did eventually retrieve the bullet-riddled moose, strapped it on their cruiser with a smirk, and drove it back to the dump.

He thought about making a run for it across the open country to the hills, but thought better of that plan. It finally dawned on him that he might be able to move faster if he ditched his 40-pound backpack, and promptly threw it into the trail. Now he just had to jump over it at every round. The moose didn't step quite so gingerly.

Finally, with Ken considering using his last shot on the moose directly, she stopped the chase and, with an air of indifference, walked off the way she had come. Luke, still sitting nearby, looked almost bored. Yukon appeared soon after with a nonchalant smile. Ken felt lucky to be alive. "I said a little thank-you prayer," he said. He held no ill will toward the beast whom his dogs had inspired to a rage. "She was probably just protecting her calf," he lamented. "I was very thankful that she didn't come right through the small evergreen. There was no doubt of her ability to accomplish that if she had a mind to."

Ken now warns others of the situation roaming dogs can present their owners while hiking and camping in Alaska. Dogs can bring other things back to camp, including bears. Although, as he was racing for the tree with the crazed moose behind him, he remembers thinking, "I might prefer to contend with a grizzly."

Killer Moose Stalked the Denali Highway

Moose are notoriously dangerous to mushers and their dog teams—especially when deep winter snows make packed trails a more attractive means of travel for the long-legged animals. In 1985, famous Iditarod musher Susan Butcher had to withdraw from the race after her team was stomped by a moose, killing two of her dogs.

Houston musher Ramey Smyth knows these dangers firsthand. A musher since childhood, he's had run-ins with moose, but never like what he experienced during a training run in 2004 on the Denali Highway.

Ramey usually carried his .357 pistol with him, but had recently loaned it to a good friend in Talkeetna who was having problems with moose on training runs. Instead, he had brought along his rifle, a 30.06. After hooking up his dogs and putting booties and coats on all, he prepared to hit the trail. That's when he realized he had forgotten the ammo. This left only his ax and a flare gun for protection. You never know what may greet you in the Alaskan backcountry.

It was desperately cold that day, with the mercury sinking to nearly 50 below. Ramey had twenty-three dogs under his control—a long string, with a heavy drag set behind them to smooth and groom the trail from where moose had punched through. He had planned to go 50 miles that day.

After about 20 miles, he approached a large hill and started the ascent. In the distance, he saw a moose on the trail. Not yet alarmed, Ramey stopped the team and tried to open his sled bag for the flare gun. But with the bitter cold, the zipper was stubborn and resisted. Meanwhile, the moose kept coming. Still Ramey pulled at the zipper. Now the moose was within 50 yards, stomping and acting aggressive. Then it charged.

Ramey quickly made the decision to move forward and called the dogs to go. He figured at least if they were moving they had a chance.

The moose was enraged, rearing up and kicking at the dogs as they began to pass. The leaders escaped blows but the swing dogs got it hard. More of the team was kicked and stomped as they continued on, leaving Ramey to finally fend off the beast.

By now he had his ice hook in hand and hit the moose in the head as he passed by. This distracted it enough to let them get ahead a little farther before Ramey stopped to assess the damage to the team.

Heartbroken, Ramey discovered one dog down and barely breathing. Its chest was caved in and death would take only a matter of minutes. This dog, Fido, was one of Ramey's best. Ramey unhooked the dog and loaded him into his sled bag, saying goodbye and telling him, "Wait for me on the other side."

A sullen Ramey now wanted to get to the top of the hill so he could turn his dogs around and head back. He needed a wide open space to pull off that kind of maneuver with such a long string of dogs. Daylight was fading.

Upon cresting the hill he couldn't believe what he was seeing. Another large bull moose, "the largest I've ever seen," he said, was occupying the trail and coming his way. He grabbed his ax and flare gun and marched about 70 yards past his dogs to meet it. Within 20 yards, he shot a flare at it. The bull barely flinched and came straightaway at him. Now the two battled within feet of each other—the moose kicking and Ramey swinging his ax. The moose kept backing him up closer and closer to his team, with neither landing a blow.

At that point, Ramey grabbed his leaders and turned them back upon the team, snaking a quick turnaround. Luckily, the moose stood motionless through this maneuver and Ramey continued back down the hill the way they had come. Darkness was now closing in.

The next 5 miles was like playing moose dodge ball, with at least five more moose jumping out at Ramey and the team as they passed by—some chasing them down the trail, some giving leeway just feet away.

Ramey would later have two more of his dogs X-rayed to find one with broken ribs and one with a fractured vertebra. Both recovered and raced again.

Asked to reflect on the events of that day, Ramey said he thinks that the moose might have been stressed because of the extreme cold temperatures and deep snow. He also says he "no longer gives moose the benefit of the doubt." "Now," he says, "I make darn sure to have a weapon with me."

Man Halts Moose Attack with Machete

On the last day of bow moose season, back in the late '80s, Tony Letuligasenoa and three friends got up early to descend upon Creamer's Field, an old dairy located in the heart of Fairbanks. This land supported a healthy population of moose, and back then no special permits were needed to hunt there.

Late that evening one of the men, Al Pavard, shot a moose. Al saw the arrow go all the way in, and though it was a good shot, they could not find the moose. Darkness was closing in.

The four men taped off the area where Al had shot the moose and decided to start again early the next morning when the daylight returned. This presented a problem, though, since bow season effectively ended at midnight that night. They decided to call Fish and Game to make sure they could return for the meat. Fish and Game officials gave their go-ahead, and the four men started out first thing in the morning.

It was decided that Tony and Terry Cox would search on the ground, while Al, a pilot, and Mike Alkana, another friend, would search for the moose from the air in Al's Cessna 150. Tony said the plane was soon in view, and he waved at them in recognition. Before long, Tony and Terry decided to fan out and were soon out of sight of each other.

The men continued their search while the plane circled overhead, with a jovial Tony waving enthusiastically every time he saw it. What he didn't know was that Terry had found the moose and the men in the plane were trying to get Tony's attention. Terry had approached within 10 yards of the moose before it stood up like it had never been hit and charged him. Terry took two steps back before getting hit and fell to the ground with the angry moose just above him.

In one daring move, Terry grabbed the moose's antlers as it came down to gore him. The moose quickly scooped him up with his nose while Terry grabbed hold of the other antler with his free hand. He was now straddling the moose's nose and was hanging on for all he was worth, screaming for Tony at the top of his lungs.

At last, Tony heard the screams. His first thought was that Terry had walked into a trap or had run into a bear. He said he'd never heard a scream like that—it was the scream of someone in serious trouble. "It sounded like a man dying," Tony said.

All Tony had on him was his machete. With forearms the size of small trees and standing 5 feet 10 inches and a sturdy 300 pounds, Tony must have made quite an impression with the machete at his side. His Samoan heritage made carrying a machete not unusual, although the others teased him for it. Neither Terry nor Tony had any other weapons with them.

When Terry came into view, Tony couldn't believe what he was seeing. There was Terry, hanging onto the antlers of the moose while it was trying to fling him to the ground and finish him off. Terry was screaming, "Kill the SOB, Tony! Kill him! Kill him!"

Tony pulled out his machete. While making sure Terry was out of the way, he made a quick motion with his knife toward the side of the moose, but it turned and knocked Tony to the ground. He promptly landed on his machete, which sliced deep into a finger, spewing blood from his leather glove. The jab never made it through the thick hide of the moose, and the long machete had bowed with the force.

Meanwhile, the men inside the plane were going crazy. They proceeded to make SOS calls to the airport and were trying to raise Fish and Game on the radio to advise them that two men were down and being gored by a moose.

Back on the scene, Terry was still screaming from atop the moose's snout, and Tony was underfoot the wild beast with a nearly severed finger. Heart pumping, adrenalin peaked—now he was determined to kill the beast. He saw how his machete had not even pierced the hide of the moose and now thought his best hope might be a leg. But as he got close, the moose spun around, following him. Tony raced to the other side of the moose and in one quick swipe, cut the moose's leg clean off.

The moose fell with Terry still hanging on and yelling. Now with Terry's help, and because of the way it fell, the moose's neck was bowed back, allowing Tony a chance to go in for a kill. He sliced its neck three or four times before the moose stopped moving.

Remarkably, Terry came out of the ruckus with only ripped hip waders and lots of black and blue marks across his entire body. Tony's finger was saved from complete disconnect by his leather glove, but he still needed medical attention. Within minutes their friends arrived with armed Fish and

Game officials in tow. They didn't know what to think of the situation and asked the men if either one had a tag! Neither Terry nor Tony had a moose tag on them. They explained they had just come out to collect the meat and could luckily point to calling Fish and Game the night before. All men were licensed hunters.

The man who shot the moose, Al Pavard, had his tag, but he wasn't the one who actually killed the moose, leaving the officials puzzled over what to charge the men with, if anything. An entry hole from the arrow was located and, upon cutting up the moose, the other half of the arrow was found in the lungs, confirming that this was the moose shot the night before.

Looking back, Tony recalls that seeing his friend atop the moose's nose was the "most amazing thing I've ever seen." He can't imagine how a moose at full strength might have fought back in that same situation. The power of that injured moose was eye opening.

No charges were ever brought against the men, as they had followed all hunting regulations to the letter. In regards to the killing, they had rightly defended their lives. No one teases Tony about his machete anymore.

8

Alaskan Treats and Eats: The Wisdom of Fishing and Homemade Wine

We Alaskans are hunters and gatherers. We take pride in stocking our own freezers and putting up our own jams. But there's more to it than that. These things are sacred. I learned that fishing is best shared with a close friend who tells lies just as well as you, or flings their lure in your general direction as soon as you get a hit. And picking berries is calming (as long as you have a gun). Spring spruce-tip tea is refreshing, homemade wine is a must, and sea urchin roe is tasty on Ritz crackers. Welcome to some of nature's best edible gifts in Alaska.

THE WISDOM OF FISHING

After a long winter, nothing beats packing up for the first fishing trip of the season. What a great feeling—the zing of the fly line, the sight of that first fish jumping in the air, the smell of the ocean, snow-capped mountains hugging the harbor in a rosy glow at midnight, ice cold feet in rubber hip waders, the taste of fresh fish in a skillet with onions, tired bones resting easily in a camp chair beside a crackling campfire—it happens just like this and you know it. Except for the wind, rain, rock-hard sleeping arrangements, and the incessant hum of predatory bugs.

Such moments are best appreciated with a friend. I realized this one day while I was fishing.

"Hey, I just had a hit!" I said.

"Hey, me too!" my friend replied.

Oddly enough, this happened throughout the day. Finally, with no fish to show for all these "hits," I realized this essential truth: you can never have a hit alone. Your buddy always has to have one too—especially when the first fish is yet to be caught. It's a very special bond. All these hits, whether real or imagined, are tallied in each angler's mind. Careful count is observed out of the corner of the eye.

Humility and compassion are also traits of a great fisherman. Fishing can really bring out the best in you. A recent outing sticks in my memory.

"Wahoooo!" I hollered as I hooked a fish. "It's big!"

My friend hadn't had any luck yet, so as I battled the fish I made sure to give him a good show—I didn't want him to feel left out, like he wasn't any good. I reeled this way and that, let the fish pull me downstream, the typical stuff (there's the humility). I could tell he really appreciated it, too. And when the fish jumped up and spit out my hook, my friend made me feel loads better by telling me what a small fish it was anyway—that it looked more like bait than a fish (there's the compassion). I don't know if he saw my hand gesture or not.

If you fish long enough, you come to realize that it's the experience of fishing that really matters, not the final fish count. I recently tried to share this theory with my friend. He had just caught a beautiful grayling. We hadn't had much luck all day (I hadn't caught a dang thing) and it was almost time to pack it up.

"Hey, that's a pretty nice fish!" I remarked. "Just look at that beauty!" (You have to build them up before you tear them down.) "It's just too bad you have to let it go." A puzzled look crossed his face. I could tell he wanted to keep the fish. He wanted to take it home. But that's not what fishing is about, and as a friend, it was my responsibility to explain this.

"I mean, come on. It's almost dark. And that little guy is hardly worth the work of cleaning." I looked at the fish and then at my friend. "Besides, it's just being here that counts, right? It's the moment. That's what it's all about."

My friend stared down at the fish.

It was working. He was about to let the fish go.

"Yeah, I suppose you're right," he said.

"Well, you better hurry up," I said nervously.

"Yeah."

And with that, he let the fish slip back into the water. I breathed a sigh of relief. I had finally gotten through to him. I looked at both of our empty creels and smiled. It's definitely the experience that counts.

The day was slowly giving way to Alaskan twilight as we made our way back to the truck. We crossed one last stream, and my friend said, "I bet there's some nice grayling in here."

"Wanna give it a quick try?" I asked.

"OK," he said.

We pulled out our rods and made a few casts in silence.

"I think I just had a hit," he said.

"Me too!" I lied.

WHO SAYS YOU CAN'T CATCH HALIBUT FROM A KAYAK?

When Howard McKim moved to Ketchikan from California five years ago to start a kayak fishing tour business, he certainly had his critics. He was repeatedly told he was crazy. Even Fish and Game didn't think he could pull it off.

According to Howard, to drop a line from a kayak puts you right in the thick of things—puts you inches from the action. You can fight a fish right under your nose. You can land it easily and put it right on the deck of your kayak and paddle it home. You can float among the sea otters and watch eagles flying overhead and connect with the earth. But most importantly, you can avoid the seasickness associated with regular charter boat fishing.

Howard's business focuses mainly on salmon fishing, but what he really enjoys is catching the "big ones." He came to Alaska with the express purpose of catching a huge halibut and making the front page of the paper. When that eventually happened—he landed a 100-pound and then a 183-pound halibut—he says the experience was surreal.

Howard uses very light tackle to fish these flat-swimming beasts. Unlike the heavy, short rods and line that pits muscle against muscle in traditional halibut charter fishing, he uses salmon rods with 15-pound test line and light reels. He says kayak fishing is more patience and finesse. And when you catch a big one, you get to take the "Ketchikan Sleigh Ride." This is what Howard calls being pulled around by a hooked fish. He says a halibut can pull you faster than you can paddle yourself.

When Howard hooked the 183-pounder, it was over an hour before he even got a look at it under his kayak. He knew it was big when it hit. He was by himself and he admits that he drifted out farther into open water than he really felt comfortable. In order to navigate, Howard put the pole between his knees and paddled that direction—same as he does with any fish. Sometimes he turns the rod around so that it's sticking out behind him, anchored under his arm while he paddles. He says you can basically get a halibut to swim with you. It took him two hours to reach the beach where he was camping with the fish in tow. "Once you catch a big fish like that, you are pretty much done for the day because it will take you all day to deal with it," McKim says. Of this big fish's fight, he says, "I've fought better."

Landing it presented an entirely different set of challenges. He wasn't even going to attempt to land it out on the water because of its size. When he reached the beach, he jumped out and immediately gaffed the fish, gave it a whack on the head, and began dragging it as far onshore as he could. By then it was really flopping around. He basically jumped on it and they started wrestling. "There was no way I was going to let that fish get back to the water and swim away," he says. "I had to get it home and show the locals."

He did manage to finally dispatch the giant fish and got it strapped to the top of his kayak. Then he broke camp and paddled back to his house on the beach. The next obstacle would be the stone stairs leading up to his house from the beach. After managing that, he stuffed the giant fish into the bed of his truck and drove it down to the dock to have it weighed.

It wasn't long before a crowd of onlookers were swarming the scales and asking about his kayak catch. "I was vindicated," Howard says. He's become known around town as "that guy who catches halibut from his kayak."

But where do you go after a catch like that? "Well, I want to try to catch a salmon shark," Howard says. "But if I find out they will attack the boat at all, I'm not going to mess with it."

For more about Howard McKim visit his website (*www.yakfishalaska.com*).

BERRY PICKING

Ah, the sweet summer season's original jewel has to be the wild berry. No matter where you live, berries can be found. Some berries are just right off the branch, while others are best in pies or made into jams. No matter what, though, berries are an excellent source of vitamins and minerals and picking is a fun way to enjoy the great Alaska outdoors and converse with a good friend. Just pick your berries wisely. If you're not sure what it is, don't pick it. You've already got bears to worry about, so don't go and get sick too.

Where to Pick

Just go for a walk. Sooner or later you'll happen upon a berry patch of some kind. Some very generous people might tell you good areas to pick berries, but probably not their "honey spot." The Alaska Cooperative Extension Service is also a good source of information about the characteristics of good berry-picking places (907-474-1530, *www.uaf.edu/coop-ext*). Just don't pick alongside a road or in any area where you suspect pesticides might have been used. Road dust also covers roadside berries, leaving an unsavory product.

How to Pick

There are better ways to pick more than just "one at a time." Nowadays you can buy a "berry rake" that will make the job much faster. It's like a square scoop with tines on the front. You just run this through the branches and the berries are scooped into the container, many at a time. This type of rake only works with single-celled berries like blueberries, cranberries, huckleberries, etc. If you try to use it with multicelled fruits like raspberries or blackberries, you'll crush them.

One of the only drawbacks of using a berry rake is the amount of residual matter collected along with the berries, like leaves and twigs. These can be easily winnowed out by dumping your berries from container to container in a strong wind, in front of a fan, or on the boat ride back to camp. If your harvest is wet, you can roll the berries down a towel into a container and the leaves and twigs will stick to the towel.

If you are going to pick without a rake, though, I like to take an old ice-cream pail with me—or anything that has a handle. You can attach the pail to a belt so that you don't set it down and step on it, spilling the whole lot that you just picked. You can rig a coffee can in the same way.

It is said that old Eskimo women used to use a *qallutaq*—a flat, wooden spoon—to beat the berry bushes, the effect being that berries would fall into their birch-bark baskets—surely the fastest way to fill a barrel full of blueberries.

BERRY FUN FACTS

- A gallon of berries weighs in at about 5 pounds.

- Fairbanks ice cream company Hot Licks Homemade Ice Cream buys around 2,000 pounds of blueberries annually for their blueberry ice cream. They pay around $4 a pound for fresh Alaska blueberries. Call 907-479-7813 for more information on selling your berries.

How to Freeze Berries

The best way to freeze these fruits is to place them in a single layer on cookie sheets and freeze them until firm. Then they can be poured into plastic freezer bags for longer storage. If berries are just poured into a bag and frozen that way, you will essentially have a solid berry block when you take it out of the freezer, as some berries will have crushed and the juices will have meshed all the berries into one. Freezing them whole on cookie sheets first avoids this problem.

COMMON ALASKAN WINE-MAKING INGREDIENTS

Birch sap

Blueberries

Clover

Cranberries

Crowberries

Currants

Dandelions

Fireweed petals

Raspberries

Rhubarb

Rose hips

Rose petals

Salmonberries

Sources for Identification and Recipes

Alaska Wildberry Guide and Cookbook, **by Alaska Geographic Society**
This book has good color illustrations and descriptions of Alaska's berries as well as an excellent section of recipes for everything from breads, to jams, to wine.

Alaska's Wild Berries and Berry-like Fruit, **by Verna E. Pratt**
This is a nice pocket-sized reference guide for identifying berries in the field.

Cooking Alaskan, **by Alaska Northwest Books**
This wonderful resource contains a section on berries and canning.

HOMEMADE WINE

Long summer days and endless winter nights make for some excellent wine-making opportunities here in Alaska. Wildflowers and berries are easily found all over the state, so a good wine is potentially growing right outside your back door. It's also fun and energizing to gather ingredients in the summer sun that will eventually be turned into wine in the winter, when you might have more time or, let's face it, be desperate for entertainment.

Wine making has been around for a long, long time. All you need is some kind of fruit or plant material, sugar, yeast, and water. The first step is mixing the sugar and fruit or plant material in a sterilized container. This sits for a few days or up to a week, occasionally stirred. Next, the mixture is strained through a sieve or cheesecloth until only the juice remains. Then, the juice is transferred into the fermentation jug where it must sit to ferment, usually for months. After the mixture stops fermenting, it is siphoned from the fermenting jug and transferred into smaller wine jugs. Then comes more sitting—a few more months for the wine to clear and develop a final flavor. It's not an overnight process, but one that, with patience, is rewarding.

CRANBERRY LIQUEUR

3 quarts lowbush cranberries

6 cups sugar

3 cups water

1 fifth of 190-proof alcohol (Everclear)

A 1-gallon stainless-steel, glass, or earthenware pot

Sieve and cheesecloth

- Crush the berries in the pot and let stand for 24 hours. Add the alcohol, cover, and let stand for another 24 hours.

- Separate the juice and alcohol from the berry pulp. Put the solution through a sieve and then into a bag made up of 3 layers of cheesecloth. Take your time and get every drop of that liquid. Discard the pulp.

- Now cook the sugar and water to make a clear syrup. Skim the surface of any scum that appears during the cooking. Cool the syrup.

- Mix the syrup and alcohol solutions together, stirring well. Bottle the liqueur, cap, and set aside to age for a minimum of 3 months. This recipe should give you 3 fifths of liqueur to set aside and just a small amount to taste right away. Ah!

From Lowbush Moose (And Other Alaskan Recipes), *by Gordon R. Nelson*
© *1978, with the permission of Alaska Northwest Books®,*
an imprint of Graphic Arts Center Publishing Company.

Alaskan Wine-Making Books

Alaska Backyard Wines, by Jan O'Meara

The Alaskan Bootlegger's Bible, by Leon W. Kania

Cooking Alaskan, by Alaska Northwest Books

Wine-Making and Homebrewing Suppliers

Arctic Brewing Supply Inc.
5915 Lake Otis Parkway #3
Anchorage, AK 99507
800-770-BREW
info@arcticbrewingsupply.com
www.arcticbrewingsupply.com

Gourmet Alaska—Nugget Mall
8745 Glacier Highway, Suite 362
Juneau, AK 99801
800-785-2665
GourmetAK@netscape.net
www.gourmetalaska.com

The Homebrew Shop
1562 Homer Spit Road
Homer, AK 99603
907-235-1470

Kenai Brewing Supplies
6383 Kenai Spur Highway
Kenai, AK 99611
866-283-2739
kenaibrewingsupplies@alaska.com
home.gci.net/~kenaibrewingsupplies

Start a Wine-Making Club and Host a Wine Tasting

If you yearn to be highfalutin, but not really, start your own wine-tasting club with this catch: members have to make their own wine. This will call in all the do-it-yourselfers, groovy hipsters, and homegrown winos while squashing the very idea that you can't wear Carhartts and flip-flops to a wine tasting

First of all, gather a group of enthusiastic friends and begin the wine-making process, with each person picking a different wine to make. The group's purpose will be to share common wine-making equipment, meet each month to give each other encouragement, and discuss and solve any problems with the process. (Not including your kitchen counter looking more like a liquor store than a fruit stand.) Of course, the club meetings can also become social events where friends and neighbors get to know each other better, and may evolve into discussions of appropriate firearms to use for dispatching insulation-stealing squirrels or whether or not the local hardware store stocks bait *and* snacks.

While the club's own wines are in the waiting or "racking" period, members can bring bottles of store-bought wine to the meetings for tastings. Each member should bring a bottle of wine within the predetermined boundaries set by consensus of the club members the month before. For instance, one month you could host a tasting of Chardonnay wines under $15. The following meeting, wines with animal names, or wines from your illegal years (Boonesfarm, Purple Passion, etc.).

The big event for the club comes when members get to taste their own homemade wines or liquors. After the tasting, recipes can be shared and plans can be made for starting next year's batch of wines!

Ingredients for a Successful Tasting

- Wrap each bottle in brown paper and assign it a number.

- Make sure there are enough glasses for everyone. If you don't have enough, ask members to bring their own special glass.

- Separate red and white wines and provide a dump bucket near each table for discards.

- Give each member a scorecard. Ask them to put their names at the top and rate each wine with a score of 1–10. Comments are encouraged.

- Let members pour their own, but suggest limiting it to a taste so there is enough to go around.

- Provide pitchers of water for rinsing glasses between wines.

- Cheese and bread go good with wine and also help to cleanse the palate. Members can bring other snacks too.

- Tally up the scorecards so that the big winner and loser wines are revealed. Scorecards are returned to members so they can keep track of which wines they liked.

- Keep a supply of sleeping bags handy for passing out on the floor.

SOME WORDS FOR DESCRIBING WINES

Almonds

Apples

Berries

Chalky

Fleeting flavor

Grapefruit

Herbs

If choking were good, this would be great

Long-lasting taste

Pears

Pepper

Smoky

Spicy

Stinky feet

Woodsy

ALASKA BEER FESTIVALS AND COMPETITIONS

If you like to try different kinds of beer or are interested in making your own and then showing it off, plan on attending one of these Alaskan Beer Festivals.

Great Alaska Beer and Barley Wine Festival
Where: Egan Center, Anchorage
When: January
What: Beer tasting of over 175 varieties from regional brewers, with entertainment and beer competition
Information: 907-562-9911, *showpros@alaska.net*, *www.auroraproductions.net/beer_n_barley.html*

Great Alaska Craft Beer and Homebrew Festival
Where: Haines
When: End of May
What: Beer tasting, entertainment, competition
Information: PO Box 385, Haines, AK 99827, 907-766-2476, *seakfair@aptalaska.net*, *www.seakfair.org*

Alaska State Fair Homebrew Competition
Where: Alaska State Fairgrounds, Palmer
When: August
What: A Beer Judge Certification Program (BJCP) sanctioned competition allowing categories of beer, cider, and mead
Information: 907-745-4827, *info@alaskastatefair.org*, *www.alaskastatefair.org*, or visit *www.bjcp.org* and click on "Scheduled competitions."

For a complete listing of beer related events in Alaska visit: *www.mosquito bytes.com/Den/Beer/Events/Events.html*.

MAKE YOUR OWN TEA

With all the bounties that the midnight sun provides, ingredients for making your own tea grow in every crack and crevice. Flower petals, dried berries, or even cultivated herbs from the garden are all potentially tasty. All it takes is a little imagination to concoct a tea that will inspire and sustain you through the long winter months—that and a little time gathering and drying the harvest.

The smells in your cup will remind you of the summer soon to come. It couldn't be easier than walking out your front door.

Ingredients

Some tea-making ingredients that can be found growing wild in Alaska

Blueberries	Nettles
Cloudberry fruit and leaves	Pineapple weed
Clover	Raspberry fruit and leaves
Fireweed petals	Rose hips
Hemlock twigs	Rose petals
Labrador tea leaves	Salmonberry leaves
Lingonberries or lowbush cranberries	Spruce tips (bright green new growth in spring)
Mint	Strawberry fruit and leaves
Mountain bluebell leaves	Yarrow

Other ingredients can be found at groceries, herbal suppliers, or health food stores:

Alfalfa	Fennel
Anise	Ginger
Cardamom	Lemon or orange peel
Chamomile	Licorice root
Cinnamon	Pepper
Cloves	

Gathering

Caution must be exercised when picking to ensure that you can positively identify the species and not pick any toxic or protected plant. Only pick things that you are sure are edible. Also, many leaves contain traces of toxins in the wilted form. Make sure to use fresh leaves or dry the leaves completely before using. Pick away from roadsides to avoid road dust and potential pesticides. And never overpick an area. Leave some plants for propagation and for other gatherers. Some plants may need to be washed to clean off dirt or dust. Just rinse under water and shake off excess or pat dry with paper towels.

Drying

To dry herbs or leaves, choose a warm dry place with good air circulation and hang plants out of direct sunlight, as the sun's rays will damage the plant's color and valuable nutrients. In Interior Alaska, this is an easy task. Tie the herbs in bunches and hang in an attic, in a greenhouse, or underneath the eaves of a house. To avoid dust accumulating on your drying herbs, place them in a small paper bag that has been sufficiently pock-marked with holes to allow air circulation. Some herbs dry well in a single layer on cookie sheets and covered with paper towels to keep dust off.

In the Southeast, your herbs may need an oven. Place herbs in single layer on a mesh screen (pizza screens work well) or a cookie sheet and place in a 100- to 125-degree oven with the door partially open. Watch closely; when the herbs are dry, take them out immediately. To test for dryness, crumble herbs between your fingers. If they break easily and crumble, they are dry. If they flex or bend at all, they need more drying time. If herbs are not completely dry, they will mold.

Berries are dried in much the same way as herbs, but take much longer to dry completely. Once dry, they can be chopped or ground up and added to the teas for an extra dose of vitamin C and a tasty zing.

A dehydrator can also be used for drying.

Storing

Package all herbs in separate containers and label. Store in tightly covered containers out of direct sunlight.

Making Tea

In general, use 1 teaspoon—more or less to taste—of herb per 1 cup of water. Double that if using fresh ingredients. You can use an infusion tea ball for your herbs, or add them directly to a pot of water and then strain before drinking. Add herbs to boiling water, and then turn off heat and let steep for 5 minutes. Herbs and herb mixes can also be packaged in tea bags. Although more time-intensive, packaging your herbs in tea bags makes for easy brewing and nice gifts.

SPRUCE-TIP TEA

Gather fresh new spruce tips in the spring. Add a handful to a pot of boiling water. Turn off heat and steep for 5 minutes. Add Labrador tea leaves and a shot of brandy or cognac for an extra kick. Strain and enjoy.

SPRITZER ICED TEA

Add ice and sparkling water to your favorite tea for a refreshing pick-me-up.

SUN TEA

Fill a gallon jar with water and add your favorite herbs and/or dried berries. Let sit in the sun all day, then strain and add sweetener if you'd like. Tea brewed this way is my favorite—very mild and smooth. Try pineapple weed, spruce tips, and Labrador tea leaves.

RASPBERRY-RHUBARB HOT SPICED TEA

4 cups wild raspberries	1 teaspoon nutmeg
4 cups thinly sliced rhubarb	Cheesecloth
2 cups water	1 cup sugar
3 sticks cinnamon	2 tablespoons lemon juice
12 whole cloves	4 cups freshly brewed tea

- In a saucepan, cook the raspberries, rhubarb, and water together with the cinnamon, cloves, and nutmeg (tied in cheesecloth). Let simmer for 5 minutes. Strain through cheesecloth in a colander. Reheat liquid with the sugar, lemon juice, and tea, stirring to dissolve the sugar. Serve hot.

Reprinted with the permission of Donning Company Publishers from
Cooking in Alaska: The Land of the Midnight Sun, *by Pat Babcock and Diane Shaw.*

BERRY GOOD CINNAMON TEA

2 sticks cinnamon

½ cup dried rose hips

¼ cup dried raspberry leaves

¼ cup dried strawberry leaves

- Add herbs to a pot of boiling water or a full tea kettle. Remove from heat and steep for 5 minutes. Strain and enjoy.

Resources for Tea Making

Alaska's Wilderness Medicines, Healthful Plants of the Far North, by Eleanor G. Viereck

A good reference, though less comprehensive than *Discovering Wild Plants* (below).

Discovering Wild Plants, by Janice J. Schofield

The ultimate guide on edible plants and their uses, by an author from Homer, Alaska. You'll find descriptions, color pictures, medicinal uses, historical uses, cosmetic uses, food uses, and toxicity warnings for plants from all over Alaska, western Canada, and the Pacific Northwest. Interesting recipes are scattered throughout too; I especially enjoy the Spice Tea recipe.

ALASKA'S FARMERS MARKETS

You probably don't think of farms when you think of Alaska. But Alaska has a long history of agricultural success, dating back to the era of the gold rushes. By necessity, the prospectors began to plant gardens to grow their own food because fresh fruit and vegetables were scarce and expensive. By the 1930s, commercial food production was in full swing in the Tanana Valley near Fairbanks. Farmers with large greenhouses and crops were providing hundreds of tons of produce to the local area each year. But it wasn't until Franklin Roosevelt's administration created the Federal Emergency Relief Administration in 1935 that Alaska's real farming potential was tapped. Over two hundred families signed up for relocation from Michigan, Wisconsin, and Minnesota to the new Matanuska Valley farming colony in Southcentral Alaska. Families were given 40 acres of land with which to cultivate and start a farm. The success rate of the program was small, but to this day Alaska continues to provide its residents with fresh produce and high-quality meats and dairy products.

These farmers, alongside hobby farmers, can be found selling their goods at farmers markets around the state—good places to find vendors selling homemade food products and craft wares. For Alaskans looking for a fresher alternative to grocery store produce, the farmers market is the place to go.

Judging by the size of the crowds that invade the markets each week, Alaskans are more than happy to support their local farmers and craftsmen. The lively market atmosphere is also sometimes enhanced by local musicians. And the quality of the products brings smiles to the faces of visitors and locals alike.

The two biggest farmers markets in the state are in Anchorage and Fairbanks. Other smaller communities like Homer, Kenai, Wasilla, and Delta Junction have markets too, just not on the scale of the bigger cities. Don't miss the opportunity to stop by any of these markets if you are passing through.

Anchorage Farmers Market
Where: 3150 Mountain View Drive
When: May–October, Saturday, 9:00 a.m.–2:00 p.m.
What: Only Alaska-grown vegetables and products. No crafts, no crowds.

Anchorage Downtown Market and Festival
Where: Downtown, 3rd Avenue, between C and E Streets
When: May 13–September 10, Saturday and Sunday, 10:00 a.m.–6:00 p.m.
What: Alaska-grown produce, seafood, arts and crafts, food, music, gifts, vendors.

Homer Farmers Market
Where: Ocean Drive, Homer
When: June–September, Saturday 10 a.m.–2 p.m., and Wednesdays in July, 4 p.m.–6 p.m.
What: Alaska-grown produce, arts and crafts, homemade goods, gifts.

Tanana Valley Farmers Market
Where: 2600 College Road, corner of College and Caribou Way, Fairbanks
When: May–September, Saturday, 9:00 a.m.–4:00 p.m., and Wednesday, 11:00 a.m.–4:00 p.m.
What: Alaska-grown produce and products, artists' wares, homemade goods, gifts, food, live music.

For a complete listing of Alaskan farmers markets, visit *www.dnr.state.ak.us/ag.*

WILD MUSHROOM MADNESS

This state is a hunter and gatherer's dream. And if you like mushrooms, you're in for a treat. Nothing beats freshly picked mushrooms sautéed in a pan of butter straight from the field.

Especially if they are morels.

In 2004, over 6.5 million acres of Interior Alaska burned—a record. It was hard not to notice the scars that the fires left on the land, but almost impossible to dismiss the frenzy that was gathering in anticipation of the potential harvest of morel mushrooms that would follow this devastation. Morels thrive in burned areas, and momentum for a substantial mushroom harvest was gathering as early as March 2005.

The Alaska Cooperative Extension Service started putting on workshops in rural communities, instructing would-be pickers about where to look and how to pick, dry, and market the mushrooms. South-facing slopes and hotly burned soil where only ash remained were said to be good places. Pickers were advised to stay away from boggy or wet areas and were told that the mushroom grows on the soil, not on decaying matter on the forest floor. Above all, fungi fruiting conditions were going to be directly dependent on the weather. Morels like very warm periods followed by good soaking rains and more warming. It was anybody's guess if the weather would cooperate.

As soon as the snow melted and temperatures started warming, all was abuzz with the coming "'shroom boom," with speculations of a second gold rush and rumors that buyers might pay up to $10 a pound for fresh mushrooms.

Locals and pro pickers from Oregon and Washington were soon staged and ready to go, as were buyers from major fungi companies. Spurred by the history of another major burn in 1991 and the subsequent mushroom harvest of over 300,000 pounds, everyone was anxiously awaiting word of mushrooms being found.

Eventually things picked up, and one Mexican crew—called the Red Van Crew because of their ride—started to consistently bring in 400 to 500 pounds of mushrooms a day. They walked 3 to 5 miles off the road just to reach the patches where they were picking, easily walking over 10 miles of backcountry a day. They eventually started bringing out even bigger loads of 600 to over 1,000 pounds of morels at a time, lining their pockets thick with cash. At one point, Tok buyers were paying up to $8 a pound, but that eventually leveled out to around $4 a pound. The Red Van Crew pulled out on July 14 and most of the other pickers and buyers were gone by then too.

It's estimated that the buyers in the Tok area bought over 150,000 pounds of morels in 2005.

Fairbanks-area pickers didn't fare quite so well. Picking was spotty at best, and a buyer at the Chatanika Lodge north of Fairbanks left mostly empty-handed after five weeks of waiting. Area pickers, if they were finding any morels, weren't sharing or selling. I ventured out in the Boundary Fire area near Chatanika and found only a handful myself.

I'm going to be back on the prowl again next year, though, as morels are definitely my favorite mushroom. And who's to say that the morels only grow the year after a burn? I've found them two to three years after a burn passed through an area, so all is not lost. Those morels are like gold, and any good prospector knows that if you're going to be successful, you've got to be persistent.

Tips for Picking and Storing Morels

- Look in an area that has recently burned.

- South-facing slopes are good.

- Start to look in late June through July, soon after rains.

- Carry morels in baskets, buckets, or paper bags. Don't leave them in plastic bags or they will melt and mold. Allow good air circulation.

- When picking, leave a portion of the stem. Pinch off with fingers or cut with a knife.

- If the mushrooms have worms, soak in salt or lemon water. Worms will crawl out of mushrooms and float to top.

- Process the mushrooms immediately after picking to avoid degradation of the product.

- Drying is the best method for preserving mushrooms. String with needle and thread and hang to dry. Or, on a breezy hot day, I've dried them on the hood of our truck on some paper in less than a couple hours. You could also use a dehydrator. Just make sure they dry quickly, or mold will form. Don't package them until you are sure they are completely dry.

- Store morels in a tightly covered container. Morels can be stored for years.

- To reconstitute morels, just soak in some water for an hour or so before use. Use the morel-infused water in your recipe too.

- As always, when venturing out in Alaskan backcountry, make sure someone knows where you are going and when you expect to return.

- Keep an eye on where you've wandered so you don't get lost, and scan the perimeter occasionally for bears or other wild animals.

- Don't pick or eat anything you can't positively identify as edible.

The Mushroom World Beyond Morels

If you're a mushroom lover, there are plenty of kinds worth pursuing in Alaska. Here's a short list of some of my favorites:

- Puffballs—easy to identify.

- King bolete—tastes like filet mignon!

- Sulfur shelf, or chicken of the woods—tastes like chicken!

Never try to identify a mushroom without first consulting a field guide or tagging along with someone who can show you what to look for. Any edible mushroom can cause allergic reactions to anyone at any time. Always try small portions of edible mushrooms first to see if any reactions occur. Afterward, prudent portions are recommended.

MUSHROOM HUNTERS' DINNER
Serves 4

> 4 tablespoons clarified butter
>
> 1 pound mushrooms, any kind, sliced or cut in chunks
>
> ½ pound cooked ham, cut in cubes
>
> One 16-ounce can whole or stewed tomatoes
>
> One 16-ounce can whole kernel corn
>
> One 16-ounce can lima beans
>
> Salt and black pepper

- Drag out that large frying pan, pour in the butter, and sauté the mushrooms until almost done. Add the ham and heat it, then add the tomatoes, corn, and beans. Stir while everything gets well heated, season to taste, and serve in soup plates.

From Lowbush Moose (And Other Alaskan Recipes), *by Gordon R. Nelson*
© 1978, with the permission of Alaska Northwest Books®,
an imprint of Graphic Arts Center Publishing Company.

FRIED CHICKEN OF THE WOODS (SULFUR SHELF)
Use your favorite batter to try this delicious mushroom that tastes like chicken! Just slice the mushroom into ¼- to ½-inch strips and batter as you would any other food. Fry until golden brown. Puffballs are also good sliced, breaded, and fried. Note: Cut and eat only the outside couple inches of chicken of the woods, as this is the freshest part—the meat tends to get tough and bitter as it gets closer to the tree.

PANFRIED MORELS
Dip rinsed morels in flour and fry in butter. Sprinkle with salt and pepper and serve. Ah!

Resources for Mushrooming

The Alaska Mushroom Hunter's Guide, **by Ben Guild**
This book has a more scientific feel and is illustrated with color drawings. Recipes included.

Alaska's Mushrooms: A Practical Guide, **by Harriette Parker**
Includes thirty-four species of mushrooms from edible to deadly, safety information, collection tips, color pictures, and recipes.

GIFTS FROM THE SEA

If you live anywhere along Alaska's coast, you will be amply rewarded if you forage for wild foods in the intertidal zone, where the sea meets the shore. Not only are sea vegetables (seaweed) usually abundant, they are nutritious and delicious as well. Historically they have been used by Native and Asian cultures as a mainstay food source, but are not traditionally valued in Western cuisine. What a shame.

Sea vegetables are easy to gather, fast growing, and can be eaten raw, boiled, fried, or dried, making them an attractive and diverse wild food.

Another prolific food source of the intertidal zone are invertebrates, or animals without backbones. These add extra nutrients and protein to the diet, and when combined with sea vegetables make for a full meal right there on the beach.

Mostly, you need not worry about poisonous species of seaweed, as the only deadly seaweed, *Lyngbya majuscula,* commonly known as mermaid's hair, favors warm, tropical waters. Other sea vegetables may be unappetizing at worst, like acid kelp or devil's apron. Northern foragers can depend largely on their palates to tell them what is good to eat and what is not, although it is always recommended to learn proper identification and taste in small amounts when trying a new wild food.

Collecting

When collecting sea vegetables, you will need rubber boots, a knife, and some kind of a collection bag. From late winter to early summer, foragers can harvest the entire plant except the holdfast (where the plant attaches itself to rocks, shells, etc.). The plant should be cut above this so that it can regenerate and grow again. As the season gets later, cut and use only the new growth. In the spring, minus or ebb tides are prime picking grounds. Sea vegetables should be harvested directly from rocks for food use. Plants higher up on the beach deposited from a storm or high tide can be used in gardens as an excellent fertilizer.

Drying

- Spread sea vegetables out on rocks on a warm, sunny day.
- Hang on clothesline.
- Dry in warm oven (150 degrees) for 10–20 minutes.
- Use a food dehydrator.

Popular Sea Vegetables

Bull Kelp: This is a very popular seaweed with many uses and is easily identified. The stipe (hollow stem) of this plant is typically sliced and pickled, but can also be used fresh or dried and ground into a seasoning. Candied kelp is also an option. This plant can be difficult to harvest from shore because it is rooted in deeper water. It is easily harvested from a boat, cutting the stem with a knife. Plants are often found on the beach after storms, but are not as fresh and not recommended for harvest.

Dulse: Typically a red or reddish-purple seaweed that extends out with fronds that look like a hand. A widely used seaweed with incredibly diverse uses, it can be eaten fresh as a snack, baked as chips, chopped for use in soups, casseroles, or omelets, or dried like jerky.

Nori: This purplish seaweed has long been a delicacy of the Japanese, who favor it for sushi. It can be chopped fresh and used in soups or salads, but is prime when dried. One particularly prized species of nori can be found growing on the stipe of bull kelp. It is noticeably red and very long and stringy. Some consider nori the finest seaweed available.

Sea Lettuce: This plant grows in thin, green sheets. Young fronds can be chopped and used in soups or dried and ground for use as a seasoning. Sea lettuce can also be boiled and served with butter or vinegar.

More Green Goodies

Beach greens (a.k.a. sea chickweed) and goosetongue, both vascular plants, are found on the beach and make excellent additions to the wild food pantry. Both are widely known and enjoyed. Goosetongue is especially good in stir fries, and beach greens make wonderful salads. You will want to gather these plants in the spring when they are young and fresh, but you can gather enough to last you through the season and then blanch and freeze them for later use. Care must be taken not to mistake the toxic arrow grass for goosetongue, which grows in the same habitat. Always consult a field guide for proper identification.

Resource for Harvesting Sea Vegetables

Discovering Wild Plants, by Janice J. Schofield
The ultimate guide for learning about harvesting seaweed or other wild plants. I especially love two of the seaweed recipes: Land and Sea-soning (a combination of seaweed and wild plants ground and used as a seasoning) and Camping Classic (ramen with seaweed and mozzarella cheese).

Invertebrates

Sea cucumbers, chitons, limpets, and sea urchins get my vote for favorite beach proteins. Each has its own flavor and distinctly enhances the wild food diet, although some may find these animals too experimental to try. You don't have to be stranded and starving on a beach to appreciate these gifts from the sea though, only open to new tastes and experiences.

Sea cucumbers can be gutted and the meat stripped from the skin. There's not much meat on a sea cucumber, but it *is* tasty! Harvest sea cucumbers at very low tides. To clean, cut off the ends and squeeze out the insides. Split lengthwise and scrape off inner muscle meat with a knife. Use in a stir fry, soups, or stews, or boil to eat.

As an interesting side note, sea cucumbers have the ability to disgorge their digestive systems from their bodies when threatened, thus, the theory goes, confusing the predator and allowing the sea cucumber to escape harm. They can then regenerate another set of digestive organs. Those wily gut-throwing sea cucumbers.

Chitons and limpets can be pried from rocks with a knife and then roasted in their shells over a fire on a grate or added to stir fries. Neither carries the risk of paralytic shellfish poisoning. Chitons are oval-shaped creatures with eight overlapping plates on their shell. Limpets look like small pointed Chinese hats. Both can be eaten raw, steamed, roasted, or beaten with a rock to tenderize them and then fried.

One of my favorite stir fries combines goosetongue, garlic, butter, soy sauce, and limpets. Sauté garlic and limpets in butter first, until the limpets pop out of their shells, then add the goosetongue and soy sauce. Sauté another 5 minutes and serve over rice. This dish cooks fast and is easily gathered from the beach.

Sea urchins are harvested for their eggs, which are excellent when eaten raw on crackers. I was surprised to find I could eat this with no problem, and it was excellent on Ritz crackers. Some say the taste of sea urchin roe is better than that of the finest caviar. Spawning time is early spring in the Southeast. Ask locals for the best time to harvest the sea urchin "caviar," more properly known as gonads. Both male and female gonads may be eaten, but the brighter orange the color (as produced by females), supposedly the better the taste.

Follow these guidelines for gathering the roe as described in *Cooking Alaskan*, by Alaska Northwest Books: "Gathering the roe is rather like shucking a very hard-shelled, hard-cooked chicken egg—easy enough if you have a hammer. Turn the sea urchin on its back, crack the test (the protective skeleton) in several places, pull off the lower part along with the viscera, loosen the egg sac from each of its five points and scoop it out with your finger."

NATIVE DELICACIES

The Native cultures of Alaska have been subsisting on the region's plants and animals for thousands of years. Deeply rooted in history and tradition, some foods are celebrated as a special part of the Native lifestyle. Foods such as whale or walrus are enjoyed as a result of a community effort and shared among all people. Other foods are gathered by individuals and shared within the family.

Eating foods gathered from the land fosters a connection that is deep and sacred. This helps preserve the heritage of a people and promotes an appreciation of traditional values, all of which are cherished by Native communities. For indigenous Alaskans, nothing is more satisfying than garnering nourishment from natural foods that are not only healthy but enhance a biocultural connection to each other and the land.

Seal

Seal oil is considered among the best of the marine mammal blubbers for a variety of food uses. It is most commonly used as a dip for frozen and dried meats and fish. Seal oil is also used as a preservative for seasonally gathered foods such as berries or beach greens.

Seal meat is eaten in a variety of ways. Seal flippers are enjoyed fresh—either raw or boiled. Seal liver is eaten raw, frozen with seal oil, or sliced and fried.

Whale

Whale blubber is called *muktuk*. It is cut off in pieces and enjoyed fresh or rancid. The piece is chewed until the whale oil is gone, then the rest is spit out. The flavor is said to be like walnut. Whale meat is eaten raw, frozen, or cooked.

Walrus

Walrus meat is eaten in a variety of ways, including raw and air-dried. Flippers are eaten raw, boiled, or roasted. Walrus blubber is eaten raw, aged, or boiled. Undigested clams from the walrus's stomach are also cleaned, boiled, and eaten.

Fish

Several varieties of fish are eaten—smoked, dried, pickled, and canned. Fish eggs are sometimes used in Eskimo ice cream (see recipe below). "Stink heads" are the heads of salmon buried in a pit and left to ferment, then eaten.

Caribou

Caribou stomach (including the contents) may be frozen and served later with seal oil. Caribou brains are sometimes eaten raw, fried, or cooked with tongue to make a stew. Caribou ribs are enjoyed fresh roasted over a fire. Roasted caribou heads are considered a delicacy. Caribou small intestines are stuffed with strips of visceral fat, ends tied, then boiled. Cooked fat is then used as a spread like butter.

MODERN VERSION OF ESKIMO ICE CREAM (*AKUTAQ*)

1½ cups shortening, softened

1–4 bananas, mashed

2 cups fresh strawberries, cut or mashed

4 pounds mixed frozen berries

Honey or sugar to taste

1½ to 2 cups boiled, flaked fish (optional)

- Beat shortening by hand in large bowl until it looks like white frosting, about 15 minutes. Fold in liquefied bananas, then the sweetener to taste. Gradually add strawberries, stirring well until the shortening is barely visible. The frozen berries will harden the mixture into "ice cream." If fish is used, add first to shortening, blending well until absorbed into the shortening. Follow with other ingredients. Traditional Eskimo ice cream uses reindeer fat, seal oil, salmonberries or blackberries, and sugar.

From Marge Andrews, a cultural representative at
the Alaska Native Heritage Center in Anchorage.

THE BEST ALASKAN COOKBOOKS

Cooking Alaskan, **by Alaska Northwest Books**
This is *the* book to have for genuine Alaskan recipes featuring local wild foods and animals. The book's chapters cover all of what Alaska has to offer: From the Waters, From Field and Forest, From the Earth, and From Cache and Cupboard. Also scattered throughout are interesting background information and stories.

Lowbush Moose, Smokehouse Bear, Tired Wolf, **and** *Hibrow Cow,* **by Gordon R. Nelson**
If you think cookbooks are just for recipes, well, you'd better get a hold of Nelson's set of Alaskan cookbooks. With a touch of humor, wit, and wisdom, this retired Alaska State Trooper will have you reading his cookbooks for his homespun tales as well as the homemade wonders. His recipes are garnered from four generations of Alaska Nelsons, people he's met in his travels, and fans of his books. The recipes are easy to follow and don't require special ingredients.

Best Recipes of Alaska's Fishing Lodges, **by Adela and Christopher Batin**
Here's your chance to tour some of Alaska's finest fishing lodges and come away with some recipes too.

The Fiddlehead Cookbook, Recipes from Alaska's Most Celebrated Restaurant and Bakery, **by Nancy and John DeCherney, Deborah Marshall, and Susan Brook**
A popular cookbook, with recipes gleaned from the famous Juneau restaurant. You'll fawn over the soups, sandwiches, pasta dishes, seafood specials, and oven-warmed baked goods that have earned the restaurant its fine reputation.

9

The Entertaining Alaskan: Art, Music, and Theater in the Last Frontier

Alaska is a place that sparks incredible creative stirrings in people. Because of its natural beauty, many find just living here an inspiration. I suspect long cold winters, insomniac summer nights, or small bush cabin living have something to do with igniting the flame of artistic talent that permeates our state. Art here comes in a wide array of mediums: from hangable, to wearable, to danceable, to art that's performed live and recalls our gold rush history or celebrates Native traditions. No matter, it's all up for grabs as you explore Alaska. I wouldn't be surprised if our great state inspires your own artistic talents.

MY NAME WILL BE IN LIGHTS (IN THE CORNER)

The nice thing about living in Alaska is that if you have any artistic talent whatsoever, you have a really good chance of standing out among our small population. This is not to say Alaskans' talents are subpar, just that the chances our work will appear in a museum, our film will go national, or that we'll get to open for a famous act are probably ten times more likely than anywhere else. As a singer-songwriter, I've been fortunate enough to open for a national act three times since my arrival in Alaska, and I'm no Jewel.

Most recently, I had the opportunity to meet Nanci Griffith. The Grammy award–winning artist was in town for a rare solo show, and I was to be the opener (whoever set this up had obviously been drinking). Wow! Not only would I get to meet Nanci Griffith, but I would get to perform on the same stage as her! What would I say? What would I sing?

I arrived as planned for my sound check and then I saw her. The stage manager introduced us, and I shook her hand with about as much enthusiasm as a person would greet the Ebola virus (didn't want to seem overly eager) and then proceeded with, "I got these shoes at the dump. Nice day, huh? I have a dog."

She immediately left to go smoke a carton of cigarettes, so she must have been nervous. I, on the other hand, was the essence of calm. Picture this: a feng shui master in a yoga pose circulating chi sitting next to a Zen sand garden in the company of yin and yang.

In other words, I was totally out of my element.

When it came time to take the stage in front of the packed house that paid good money to see a Nashville icon, I couldn't have been more confident. My windpipe was closing in on me, my song choice included a hit by SpongeBob SquarePants, and I suddenly remembered that I had left the iron on in my tinder-dry log cabin.

I would love to tell you that I performed well under pressure and used this tremendous opportunity to meet a legend with grace and not make a fool of myself, but alas, my genetics are set. My nerves got the best of me. Instead of gaining more confidence as my songs went on, I was most certainly hoping the stage would swallow me up along with my off-key, cotton-mouthed notes. I have never wanted to "exit stage left" faster in my entire life.

The crowd was gracious enough, and if they could only hear me singing in the car, I think they'd like me.

Nanci avoided eye contact as I left the stage, which I took as a good sign. I wanted to wish her good luck, so I said, "Boy I'm thirsty," and then she took the stage. I can only say that Nanci Griffith is a gracious, wonderful performer who deserved better than what I inflicted on her that day. Her voice was angelic and her show was fantastic.

Afterward, with not one last shred of dignity, I knocked on her dressing room door to see if I could get an autograph and a picture. After a long pause, she opened the door, signed my guitar, and posed for a picture (she's kind of smirking in the photo). I can't be sure, but her inscription either says "Sing Out!" or "Shut Up!" It's pretty cool.

MUSIC

The music scene in Alaska is alive and kickin'! I have yet to live in a place that tops this state for musical talent and the accompanying opportunities to get out there and play and/or see live music. It is just phenomenal. Whether at a community center or at a festival, or performances at a local watering hole or coffeehouse, it's easy to catch music in most any town in Alaska at most any time.

Here are a couple of publications to turn to for the most up-to-date arts and entertainment information, followed by some well-known Alaskan artists. Beyond this, take time to support local music or get involved in the music scene yourself. It pays to have something to do on dark, cold winter nights and endless summer days.

The Anchorage Press (*www.anchoragepress.com*)

"Alaska's most wired newspaper." Free Anchorage-wide art, entertainment, recreation, news, and metro features newspaper, published weekly. Also distributed in Fairbanks and covers Fairbanks events and happenings.

Fbx Square (*http://fbxsquare.com*)

"A guide to what's going on in Fairbanks." Free and published weekly.

Robin Dale Ford

You'd be hard pressed to find an album with a banjo as the lead instrument, but Fairbanks's Robin Dale Ford dazzled us all with her 2001 release, *Ain't That Skippin and Flyin*, with its melodic and lovely tunes that not only feature her excellent banjo playing, but also her angelic vocals. Check out Robin's music at 10th Planet Records (*www.10thplanet.com*).

Gangly Moose (*www.ganglymoose.com*)

If it's a jam band you're looking for, look no further than Fairbanks's Gangly Moose. To describe their sound, I offer this quote from their website: "an original mix of Funkadelic, Primus-meets-Woody-Guthrie style commonly referred to as 'cabin rock.'" Hippies love 'em.

Hobo Jim: "Alaska's State Balladeer" (*www.hobojim.com*)

It's hard to experience Alaska without experiencing Hobo Jim. This former commercial fisherman/logger/cowboy sings of his life and wilderness lifestyle in his rousing good-time, sing-along songs. I'll just put it this way: the guy's a legend and his shows are great fun.

Matt Hopper (*www.matthopper.com*)

Formerly fronting the wildly popular Anchorage band, the Roman Candles, Matt Hopper has struck out on his own and is pursuing a music life beyond

Alaska's borders, living on couches, bumming rides, and living right proper as an artist in training with the big guns. He describes his solo music as "psychedelic folk." Matt has also started somewhat of a phenomenon known as FAWM, or February Album Writing Month (*www.fawm.org*), a ritual that he began with a friend in an effort to spawn an entire record of new material in just one month. Over three hundred people have taken part so far, and every year the number gets bigger.

Melissa Mitchell (*www.homegrownak.com*)

This wildly popular Girdwood musician has been showing Alaskans the right way to groove with her smooth, soulful voice and rhythm-driven folk for over ten years. First with the band Homegrown, and then on her own with the Melissa Mitchell Band, this powerhouse of groove has been embraced by Alaskans—especially the gypsy hipsters.

Ken Peltier *(www.kenpeltier.com)*

If it's country music you like, Ken Peltier is your man. It's hard to believe this guy's from Alaska with the talent he brings to the table. If you closed your eyes and listened to him sing, you'd swear you were listening to some big star straight out of Nashville. Ken is essentially the go-to guy when big-name country acts roll through Alaska and has opened for many famous bands.

Buddy Tabor

This seasoned Juneau house painter was called "a player and a poet" by the late Townes Van Zandt. If that isn't an endorsement, I don't know what is. Sometimes blues, sometimes folk, sometimes country, this singing poet uses the color of life to paint pictures with his deeply affected voice and quality guitar finger work. Order Buddy's albums from eFolkMusic (*www.efolkmusic.org*, type his name in the search field).

Ken Waldman "Alaska's Fiddling Poet" (*www.kenwaldman.com*)

This Alaska gem is both a poet and a musician. Using squeaky old-timey fiddle tunes as the backdrop for his Alaskan-themed poems, Ken crafts the everyday experience into engaging and entertaining riffs of life, love, pain, and joy.

Jared Woods (*www.jaredwoods.com*)

This Anchorage native is steadily winning crowds over with his smooth singer-songwriter ways and in 2003 was voted Best Singer in Anchorage by the readers of the *Anchorage Press*. Jared has been compared to John Lennon and

Elliott Smith and is probably one of the few Alaskan musicians actually making a living at it—it's his day job. Make sure to see him live if you happen to be in Anchorage.

Larry Zarella/Denali Cooks (*www.larryzarella.com*)
Talkeetna musician Larry Zarella has at once a recognizable voice and an easy listening style—immediately likeable and memorable. Now mostly performing solo, Larry is one of the founding members of the Denali Cooks, a band made up of former Denali Hotel cooks that dominated Alaska throughout the '90s and remains celebrated to this day.

More Great Alaska Bands

Bearfoot Bluegrass (*www.bearfootbluegrass.com*)
Telluride Bluegrass Festival winners, from Anchorage.

Delmag (*www.delmag.biz*)
Alternative rock, from Anchorage.

Nervis Rex (*www.mcproductions.com/aska.htm*)
Ska band, from Anchorage.

Pamyua (*www.pamyua.com*)
Tribal funk and world music. 2003 Record of the Year winner at the Native American Music Awards.

Sweating Honey (*www.myspace.com/sweatinghoney*)
Eclectic danceable tunes with funk and groove, from Fairbanks.

The Whipsaws (*www.thewhipsaws.com*)
Alaska alt-country twang and stomp, from Anchorage.

Nick Jans on Timothy "Grizzly Man" Treadwell

Among the stacks of books written by Alaska's most celebrated writers, you would surely find Nick Jans's *The Last Light Breaking: Living Among Alaska's Inupiat Eskimos, A Place Beyond: Finding Home in Arctic Alaska,* and *Tracks of the Unseen: Meditations on Alaska's Wildlife, Landscape and Photography.* These books offer readers beautiful and telling essays of a life spent adventuring and discovering Alaska, with much self-examination and meditation along the way. Nick is at once a voice of reason explaining why we all live here, while also juxtaposing the realities and challenges we face as we grow attached to a land.

This is what made him the perfect person to write *The Grizzly Maze,* the much publicized story of Californian Timothy Treadwell's seemingly self-inflicted death by a brown bear at Upper Kaflia Lake in Alaska's Katmai National Park in 2003. Asked why he decided to tackle a project so unlike his previous collections, Nick replies, "I wanted this story to be written by someone from Alaska. Without the spin." Then he adds, "It's the story I'd been training for my whole life."

Indeed, Nick's straightforward, thoughtful, and "no spin" writing style has made this book stand out among sensationalized portrayals as a truthful and fascinating investigation into the life and death of Timothy Treadwell—a passionate supporter of bears who, to some extent, Nick says he can identify with. Nick left out the celebrity status that followed Treadwell and instead focused on the facts and depth of the story, neither aligning with Treadwell's naysayers nor his compatriots—though Nick researched each and gives his opinion in plenty of places. Nick was the private investigator, prosecuting attorney, defense attorney, jury, and judge—a difficult balance to maintain—and to this day, Nick admits that he doesn't know where he stands on the subject of Timothy Treadwell.

At the base of this story is a profoundly confusing man who sets out to "defend" some of the most protected bears in the world from supposed harm. His obsession of living within feet of these bears is preserved on film from over ten years of summer visits to his favorite places in Katmai, including one he called the Grizzly Maze, a deep and jungled bear habitat that was the ultimate location of his death. This man's tactics were a beacon for discontent among most Alaskans—singing to and naming bears are neither recommended nor celebrated—and many saw Treadwell as a martyr for the fairytale ideals of Outside animal preservation interests that swing wide of reality.

Nick says the book is about bear and people, with Treadwell being the lens through which to examine bear and human relations. He also notes that the book, if anything, shows just how dangerous bears are not, acknowledging that he trusts bears more than drunks or loose sled dogs in a village—the latter of which have mauled him twice. This from a man who has spent hundreds if not thousands of hours in the backcountry, with numerous bear encounters under his belt. Nick's ultimate goal was to defend the truth with this book, conceding that Timothy did morally questionable things, but indeed shared a level of interconnectedness and spirituality with the Katmai bears that you or I will probably never understand. "What kind of man would do that?" he asks of Treadwell's sleeping without protection among one of Alaska's most dense bear concentrations, relating it to "camping next to a turnstile in the New York subway."

Nick says he wants his writing to be around a hundred years from now. I suspect he wants us to pick up his books and read them with the same fervor that we do now. Judging from his track record—and his elegant, honest prose—that will be no problem.

Also an accomplished photographer, Nick's next book will explore the many facets of the wolf in Alaska, to be called *Alaska's Wolf Wars*.

Visit *www.nickjans.com* for more information.

Want to Write Like Nick Jans?

You better get some chops and sign up for the very popular Kachemak Bay Writers' Conference held every June in Homer (*http://writersconference.homer.alaska.edu*). This nationally recognized conference features workshops, readings, and panel presentations in fiction, poetry, nonfiction and also attends to the business of writing.

Live-Music Venues

ANCHORAGE

Chilkoot Charlie's (a.k.a. Koots)
2435 Spenard Avenue
907-272-1010
www.koots.com

Humpy's
610 W 6th Street
907-276-2337
www.humpys.com

Snow Goose Restaurant
3rd and G Street
907-277-7727
www.alaskabeers.com

DELTA JUNCTION

Sawmill Creek Lodge
Mile 1404 Alaska Highway
907-895-4924

DENALI NATIONAL PARK

Denali Park Salmon Bake
238.5 George Parks Highway
907-683-2733
www.denaliparksalmonbake.com

FAIRBANKS

College Coffeehouse
3677 College Road
907-374-0468
www.collegecoffeehousefairbanks.com

Ivory Jack's
2581 Goldstream Road
907-455-6666

The Blue Loon
2999 George Parks Highway
907-457-5666
www.theblueloon.com

The Marlin
3412 College Avenue
907-479-4646

GIRDWOOD

Sitzmark Bar & Grill
Alyeska Ski Resort
907-754-1111
www.alyeskaresort.com

HOMER

The Alibi
453 E Pioneer Avenue
907-235-9199

Beluga Lake Lodge and Restaurant
204 Ocean Drive Loop
907-235-5995

KODIAK

The Rendezvous
11652 Chiniak Highway
907-487-2233

PALMER

Four Corners Lounge
Mile 5.5 Palmer-Wasilla Highway
907-746-5066

SEWARD

Yukon Bar
4th and Washington
907-224-3063

TALKEETNA

Latitude 62
Mile 13.7 Talkeetna Spur Road
907-733-2262

Top 5 Alaskan Music Festivals

Though you can barely round a weekend corner on the summer calendar without bumping into a music festival, keep these five noteworthy happenings in mind (listed in order of occurrence).

Alaska Folk Fest
Where: Juneau
When: April
Cost: Free
What: Annual festival that brings together musicians from around the state to perform fifteen-minute sets of folk, bluegrass, country, pop, Celtic, old-timey, orchestral, and other musical genres on one stage in front of a capacity crowd of one thousand people. Expect anything from school groups to professionals and everything in between. On the weekend, dance sets dominate another nearby building, which features a guest caller. One nationally renowned artist is featured throughout the festival.
Information: 907-463-3316, *info@alaskafolkfestival.org, www.akfolkfest.org*

International Mini Folk Fest
Where: Skagway
When: End of April

Cost: $10

What: One day of music in Skagway, then one day of music in Whitehorse, Canada.

Information: 907-983-1898, *chamber@aptalaska.org*, *www.skagwaychamber.org*

Fairbanks Summer Folk Fest
Where: Pioneer Park
When: June
Cost: Free
What: Outdoor music festival featuring Alaskan musicians with food and craft vendors.
Information: 907-488-0556, *trudy@acousticadventures.com*, *www.acousticadventures.com*

Anderson Bluegrass and Country Music Festival
Where: Anderson Riverside Park
When: End of July
Cost: Varies, but affordable
What: Draws hippies and music lovers from around the state for homegrown music. Showers, restrooms, and RV camping available; camping is included in the ticket price.
Information: *andersonbluegrass@yahoo.com*, keep your ear to the radio for this festival, previous years' lineups posted at *www.acousticadventures.com*

KBBI Concert on the Lawn
Where: Homer
When: End of July
Cost: Varies, check website
What: Annual outdoor benefit to support public radio. Great live music by local musicians and those from around the state. Homer is Jewel's hometown.
Information: 907-235-7721, *dorle@kbbi.org, www.kbbi.org*

ALASKA NATIVE ARTS, FESTIVALS, AND EVENTS

You can't live in Alaska without witnessing the profound impact of Alaska Native art. The inescapable beauty of this art inhabits every corner of our history here, with deep cultural meanings imbedded throughout. Much historic Native art was traditionally used in practical ways or as ceremonial objects, whereas contemporary Native art is probably used more for creative expression and/or offered for sale to art collectors or tourists so that the artist can make a living. No matter, Native artisans produce an astounding body of work derived from cultural and traditional processes using natural and sometimes man-made materials. Whether made using traditional methods or more modern tools (electric drills, sewing machines, etc.), their work is revered and appreciated for the artistry displayed.

From Eskimo ivory carvings to Chilkat basketry, from Tlingit woodworking and jewelry to Athabascan skin sewing and beadwork, Native artwork abounds. Take time to enjoy and support this artwork and discover the history and stories behind it along the way. You may just be helping to support another generation of Native artisans pursuing the traditions of their forefathers and honoring the customs of their culture.

Alaska Native Heritage Center
Where: Anchorage
When: Year-round
What: Native dancing, storytelling, artists, guided tours with cultural hosts, and informative exhibits.
Information: 907-330-8000, *info@alaskanative.net, www.alaskanative.net*

Native Arts Festival
Where: Fairbanks
When: Late February or March
What: Features "artistic expressions of each Alaska Native culture," with artists, craftspeople, and dancers.
Information: 907-474-6689, *fscae@uaf.edu,*
www.geocities.com/festivalofnativearts

Celebration
Where: Juneau
When: Every other year in June
What: Celebrates and showcases Southeast Alaska Native customs and traditions through song, dance, arts, crafts, and the native languages of Tlingit, Haida, and Tsimshian tribal members.
Information: 907-463-4844, *www.sealaskaheritage.org/celebration/index.htm*

World Eskimo-Indian Olympics

Where: Fairbanks

When: June

What: Traditional Native sports, dancing, and skills events. This event provides an intimate and amazing look at a people whose skills are passed from generation to generation in the hopes of keeping social and traditional values and activities alive in an ever-modernizing world.

Information: 907-452-6646, *weio@weio.org, www.weio.org*

Athabascan Fiddling Festival

Where: Fairbanks

When: November weekend closest to Veteran's Day

What: A mainstay festival for over twenty-four years, features old-timey fiddle music mixed with singing, dancing, and over a hundred performers ranging in age from eight to eighty. Fiddle music was introduced by fur trappers and traders working for the Hudson's Bay Company in Interior Alaska and was adopted by Natives who integrated their own rhythm and drum traditions into the music. Lively dancing and audience participation.

Information: 907-452-1825, check the *Fairbanks Daily News-Miner* in November for further details.

FIRST FRIDAY IN ALASKA

The pervading assumption that Alaska is an icy realm of nothingness dotted with igloos and penguins still exists. Thankfully, this couldn't be farther from the truth. Alaska is a hotbed for artistic expression and has played host to the ever-popular notion of "First Friday" for several years now—just like what you'd expect to find in hip New York or Chicago. First Friday is the night when, once a month, gallery owners showcase new art and artists while providing the experience of a social event mixed with wine, food, and sometimes music.

Far from highbrow, all are welcome to join in the First Friday festivities. Jinx Whitaker, owner of New Horizons Gallery in Fairbanks, says the First Friday movement has taken on a life of its own since it was introduced a few years ago. It has helped to showcase the downtown area and its effects have spilled over to positively influence nearby restaurants and retail businesses as well.

My first experience with First Friday was a delightful surprise. One very cold Friday in December, a friend and I embarked on an artful journey of gallery

Get Your Laugh On at the Fairbanks Funny Festival

Have you always dreamed of being a stand-up comic but were too scared to try out your chops? Well, here's your comic Yellow Brick Road. The Fairbanks Funny Festival, which has been around for seven years, provides workshops and advice to those looking to grease their funny bones. The culmination event for the festival is a five-minute performance by the participants in front of a live audience at the Blue Loon.

Each year a full-time professional comic headlines the festival and helps teach the workshops. Local comedians and radio hosts Glen Anderson and Jerry Evans host the festival and are responsible for launching and inspiring newfound comedic talent throughout Alaska and beyond.

Due to the festival's success, a Junior Funny Festival was added to cater to the twenty-one and under set, with its final performance at Pioneer Park.

The three-day festival (nighttime workshops) is held in January at the Blue Loon in Fairbanks. Registration costs around $75 and can be done online (*www.alaskacomedy.com*) or through New Northwest Broadcasters (1060 Aspen Street, Fairbanks, 907-451-5910).

hopping in downtown Fairbanks. The dark, bitter sky was made friendly by the hundreds of twinkling white lights that framed the frosty landscape of buildings and shops as we left our vehicle running on a side street in the freezing cold.

Once inside the first gallery, it was like a Mecca for the sunlight deprived—art shining under warm lights accompanied by soft music and wine at the door. I was instantly happy. A large smile spread across my lips, and my eyes lit up like a kid at Christmas. I was enamored with the art that surrounded me—sculptures, figurines, paintings, jewelry, you name it—and even a complimentary packaged cookie so beautiful I didn't know if I should eat it. Of course I did. I shuffled about in my large parka and mukluks taking it all in, kicking myself for not being rich enough to buy anything.

Our last stop led us down the highway to Ester, a small but very artsy community south of Fairbanks. Inside there was a reception for a group of local women who had posed in their nearly-nothings for an artsy B-grade calendar that was debuting that night. I again found the food table and tasted some wonderful reindeer sausage and crackers, then washed it down with punch and chocolate.

A happy reprieve from winter, First Fridays were thereafter penciled on my calendar (not the Ester women calendar—that would be too weird) for months to come.

GOLD RUSH DRAMA, ROBERT SERVICE KNOCK-OFFS, AND GOOD TIME DANCING GIRLS–NOW THAT'S THEATER!

You might be surprised to learn that I'm not a lover of Shakespeare nor of other fine theatrical productions (how'd you like the "nor" I threw in there?). It's not that I don't appreciate professional theater; it's that taking sips of smuggled whiskey from your coat pocket during the show is usually frowned upon. I'd rather go to a show that serves spicy chicken wings with dance hall girls kicking up their heels and a man dressed as Robert Service spouting off poetry from a bygone era—maybe even see someone shoot off a fake gun in the whole mess of it. Alaska history is like that, and there is some darn good theater around the state that recreates the excitement of those gold rush days. If nothing else, send your relatives to these shows when they're in town and, at the very least, you'll be free of them for a couple hours. Here's a round-up of some of Alaska's fun-loving theater productions.

Alaska Cabin Nite Dinner Theater
Where: Denali National Park, Denali Park Resorts' McKinley Chalet Resort
When: June–August, 5:30 p.m. and 8:30 p.m. nightly
What: "True to life Gold Rush tale of adventure in early 1900's Alaska," with heroine Fannie Quigley and accompanying cast of characters. All-you-can-eat family-style meal is included. Now if that doesn't sound like fun, you need your head examined. Reservations required.
Information: 1-800-276-7234, *denali@aramark.com*,
www.denaliparkresorts.com/cabin_nite.shtml

Days of '98 Show

Where: Eagle's Hall, 6th and Broadway, Skagway

When: Daily matinees and nighttime shows

What: This one-hour historical drama of gold rush proportions "recreates the life of Alaska's most notorious con-man, Jefferson Randolph 'Soapy' Smith, who reigned over Skagway during the wild days of the Klondike Gold Rush." You gotta love that outlaw. At over seventy years running, this show boasts that it's the longest-running production of its type in the North.

Information: *www.alaskan.com/daysof98*

Golden Heart Revue

Where: Palace Theatre, Pioneer Park, 3175 College Road, Fairbanks

When: May–September, 8:15 p.m. nightly, 6:30 p.m. show added as needed

What: Don't miss a stop in the historic Gold Rush Town section of Pioneer Park in Fairbanks for this "lighthearted, comic look at the colorful characters from early and present-day Fairbanks." This fun and lively cast of characters relives the days of the gold rush in a performance that will leave you wishing that fancy dresses and carrying a gun on your hip were still fashionable. Oh wait, up here in Alaska gun slinging *is* still fashionable. Reservations recommended.

Information: 907-452-7274 or 800-354-7274, *www.akvisit.com/palace.html*

Malemute Saloon's "Service with a Smile"

Where: Ester Gold Camp, Ester, 5 miles south of Fairbanks on the Parks Highway

When: Late May–September, 9:00 p.m. nightly

What: Authentic gold-camp nostalgia dominates the scenery of this saloon, which is listed on the National Register of Historical Places. You'll feel like you're stepping back in time as you pass through the swinging doors and your feet crunch on the sawdust floor, but you'll be transfixed as you watch the professional cast recreate the fun history of the gold rush era. Robert Service, the "Bard of the North," makes an appearance here and you'll be treated to an engaging reading of his vivid poetry from that time. Pig-out at the all-you-can-eat crab buffet before the show, and plan on a night's stay at the hotel or in the campground. Reservations recommended.

Information: 907-452-7274 or 800-354-7274, *www.akvisit.com/malemute.html*

A GUIDE TO "REAL THEATER" (REVISITED)

OK, now that I've snubbed all you bona fide theater buffs and pretty much called you sissies for liking theater that doesn't include cocktail waitresses, I'll humor you with a short list of quality theater companies for which you can dress up and pretend to be cooler than me.

Cyrano's Theatre Company (*www.cyranos.org*)
This Anchorage theater company "produces professional quality dramatic works utilizing Alaskan talent." They have employed actors and technicians from Juneau to Fairbanks, often using local University of Alaska–Anchorage drama students. Nurturing regional talent is one of this company's primary goals: "In this respect, we have been a transition point from academic the-atre to professional careers." A new play debuts every month, and the improv group Scared Scriptless performs every other Saturday at 10:00 p.m. Cyrano's café is also a place to socialize after plays.

Fairbanks Shakespeare Theatre (*www.fstalaska.org/index.html*)
Every year a talented group of actors set up a stage in the birch forest of Fairbanks to present Shakespeare in an outdoor show that encompasses lively actors, innovative design, and artistic integrity. This theater company strives to bring Alaska—especially Alaskan youth—the works of Shakespeare; shows are free to those eighteen and under. When the show in Fairbanks is over, the company often travels around the state and to some locations in Canada—outdoor set and all. In 2004 over ten thousand people across Alaska and Canada watched the performance. In late January through early February the company holds its Bard-a-Thon, in which the complete works of Shakespeare are read 24-7 by volunteers. Spectators are welcome, and the readings are also commonly broadcast over the radio.

The Last Frontier Theatre Conference
(*www.pwscc.edu/conference/layout.shtml*)
Write your own play for fame and fortune! This dynamic conference takes place every year at the Prince William Sound Community College in Valdez and attracts nationally renowned theater professionals and educators to critique plays that are sent in from playwrights and selected for public readings in the conference's Play Lab. Each year between fifty and seventy plays are accepted

for the conference. Readings are performed by actors who have rehearsed the plays, and afterward the plays are reviewed by a professional panel and the audience. Such dignitaries as Edward Albee and Arthur Miller have been special guests. Other conference activities include workshops, classes, and panel discussions with the featured artists. Live plays are performed every evening, followed by music and lively interactions in what's called the Fringe Festival at a nearby establishment.

Perseverance Theatre (*www.perseverancetheatre.org*)

Founded in 1979, Perseverance Theatre was formed to serve a rising generation of American, Alaskan, and world-theater artists, to embrace artists and audiences around the state, and to explore classic and contemporary theater through an "Alaskan lens." For example, in its retelling of Herman Melville's *Moby Dick* in 2001, the theater relied heavily on the whaling experience of the Inupiat Eskimos. This Juneau flagship for professional theater in the state serves over twenty thousand artists and audiences annually through its productions, education and outreach programs, internships, statewide tours, festivals, play readings, and collaborations and is the resident theater at the University of Alaska–Southeast. For more information, theater schedule, casting, or tickets, visit the company's website.

10

True North: Everyday Alaskans, Extraordinary Stories

You never know who's got a story. Chances are if you stick around Alaska long enough, you could fill a book with incredible stories from everyday Alaskans. From making an unscheduled exit from a plane, to being attacked by a grizzly, the Alaskans in the following pages epitomize the spirit of this great land, and most importantly, they lived to tell their tales.

THEY BURNT THEIR SNOWMACHINES TO STAY ALIVE

When John Holtry and his two friends left Fairbanks on a snowy February day a few years ago for some snowmachining in the Hoodoo Mountains just north of Paxson, they could have never predicted that they would later torch those very snowmachines in a desperate bid to stay alive.

By midmorning, the three friends had arrived at a staging area at the base of the mountains for what was to be a full day of snowmachining. The day was balmy at 17 degrees Fahrenheit, and it was snowing. The men unloaded their sleds and were anxious to get going. The landscape in these mountains is breathtaking: a solid white expanse of hills, valleys, and peaks. There are no trees, save a few small scrub willows or alders. There is not a trace of civilization as far as the eye can see. It is a snowmachiner's paradise.

After about an hour of riding, it started snowing harder. The winter sun had come and gone behind the clouds, and the dim light was fading into a snowy mirage of flat light. The men were experienced riders. They were riding short to midlength track snowmachines, the kind that are better for going fast and riding packed trails. John would later tell me that the snow off the trail was waist deep.

They kept riding, but the flat light was becoming so deceiving that at times they couldn't even tell if they were moving. They had to put their feet down in order to get their bearings and eventually realized that they were no longer on the trail. Conditions had become blizzard-like. The men were so disoriented that they had to stop occasionally and get off their machines to scout ahead to make sure they weren't about to ride off a cliff.

They were heading down a valley and were getting mired in the deep, soft snow. They had to stomp down paths in front of their machines to keep them going. John recalls, "You had to gun it but then you'd only go a little ways before you were bogged down again. And you couldn't see anything because the snow was coming over the hood and the windshield."

This went on for hours, and the level of exertion required for these maneuvers was exhausting. The men hoped to get to the bottom of the valley and perhaps ride out from there. Meanwhile, the wet snow was soaking them. Nerves were wearing thin. Somewhere in all of this, one of the snowmachines hit a large boulder and the ski broke, so they had to jury-rig it to keep it going. But the snow just kept getting deeper. The men had cell phones along but no connection could be made. Before long it was dark.

Between them they had two granola bars, a few snack-size candy bars, some water, and a space blanket. They also had matches and lighters. One guy only had on a Carhartt coat, jeans, long johns, and work boots, and he was soaked and shivering. John and his other friend were dressed more appropriately in some winter gear, but they too were cold. Exhausted, wet, and hypothermic, the trio called it quits sometime after midnight.

That's when the first machine was torched.

When I asked John how they decided to burn a snowmachine, he said, "We had no other choice. There was nothing else to burn. It was either burn a snowmachine or die." When deciding whose machine was going to be burned, the one with the bad ski was voted off the hill. John says at that point, he was glad to see it go. The men huddled around the melting snowmachine and were able to dry out. It burned extremely hot, even melting the aluminum on the machine as well as one man's goggles and the back of John's own gloves. They also split the granola bars and drank some water. The fire raged for two hours before dying out.

They continued on a little farther before stopping for the night and positioned the remaining two snowmachines around them and dug a shelter in the snow. The wind had picked up and the snow was still falling. The three men lay side by side for warmth, but sleep was futile and anxiety-ridden. John got up throughout the night to jump up and down until he could feel his feet and was warm again. He thinks he did this five or six times. He tried to arouse the others to jump around and get warm, but they never moved. The friends were also using the exhaust on the snowmachines to warm their hands, but relief was only temporary. John estimates the temperature that night at 15 below, and by dawn he says there was at least a foot of new snow on the ground.

Next day, skies were born blue, and this brought slightly better spirits. The storm had passed, and the men were able to get as much water as they wanted from a small stream running the same direction they were traveling. But they were very cold and they had nothing to eat. Throughout the ordeal, no one ever broke down or suggested that they might not make it out, but tempers were short and the trio were arguing among themselves as to the best course of action. The straits were dire.

With the men being so cold, the decision was made to burn the second snowmachine shortly after they awoke. This time though, the prospect of spending another night or two in the cold was prompting the men to plan ahead. Before they burnt the second sled, they cut off the seat cover, the seat foam, and emptied some gas to take with them to be used later if needed. Again, the fire warmed the men, but they doubted anyone had seen the smoke so early in the morning so far back in the hills. Their morale was low. They were bickering and arguing about what to do next. They hadn't discussed it out loud, but at least one man was now having serious doubts as to whether they would make it out or not.

The decision was made to turn around, to back track. They wrestled the third snowmachine for a few hours, with John estimating that they probably only traveled a quarter mile before giving up. By now it was around 10:00 in the morning, and they figured maybe someone would see the smoke if they burnt the last machine. So they torched it—their last hope for a signal.

This last sled was John's, and he says it was hard to see it go up in flames. He'd only had it a short time and had spent $3,000 on it. That brought the total worth of torched snowmachines to over $10,000.

The three men continued up the valley, following the impressions of their tracks from the day before. The trio were cold and weak, but the sun had warmed the air to around 15 degrees Fahrenheit, and the daylight was boosting their spirits. Within a half hour of burning the third sled, they saw some riders at the top of the ridge. John said there was instant relief at the sight of their would-be rescuers.

The rescuers picked up the men and continued down the valley, but not without getting stuck a few times along the way. They finally merged onto a well-traveled trail and after about an hour of riding, the men were delivered back to their truck.

First thing they did was to call their families to let them know they were OK. A search had already been launched and there were riders out looking for the men. A helicopter was just about to take off when word came that the men had been found. One of John's friends had a bit of frostbite, but other than that the men survived relatively unscathed, save the loss of the snowmachines.

John bought another sled the following year and has had no trouble getting back in the saddle, although he is always prepared for emergencies now. He stays out of the hills, and his new snowmachine is identical to the one he rode out on that day with his rescuer. It's got a long track and is better in deep snow. John says the experience soured one of his friends on riding, and he doesn't go out much now. He has lost touch with the other man.

John says that he has yet to endure a more physical challenge than in that grueling thirty-eight hours. It took everything he had to persevere. But in the end, he came out alive.

PLANE DEPOSITS MAN ON RUNWAY BEFORE LANDING

When John Moore of Chugiak, Alaska, boarded the small Piper PA22 airplane on that fateful day back in August 1985, he had no idea he would make his own exit from the plane before it landed.

John and his wife, Melanie, along with two visiting friends from Michigan, had just spent a few days at Damn Creek, an old mining camp about a ten-minute flight from the tiny community of McCarthy. They had spent their days panning for gold and were enjoying the lingering days of summer, showing off Alaska to their friends. The weather was perfect, and the pilot had ferried their two friends back to the airstrip in McCarthy. When the pilot returned a second time, he told them he could only take one passenger because he was transporting some fuel and the back seats were taken out. It was decided that Melanie would be the one to fly out. The pilot told John he would be back for him in the morning. But John watched as the pilot stopped halfway down the runway and turned around. He opened his door and told John that if he wanted to get in back with the fuel, he would take him now. John agreed and was soon crouched down in between the fuel barrels sitting on his heels, arms around his knees.

This wasn't such a big deal. The flight was only ten minutes, and John reasoned that the inconvenience of not having a seat was better than waiting another day for a pick-up. The skies were clear and the flight was perfect. As the runway came into view, the pilot banked the plane hard as he rounded the far end of the runway to get into position to land. This maneuver was so smooth that John never realized the plane was banking. His vision was obstructed by the fuel barrels and he never had a notion to steady himself. He sat the same as he had for the entire flight—on his heels, arms around his knees.

The centrifugal force was enough to keep him in place while the plane's wings were one up, one down in the turn. But when the plane was righted, John wasn't ready for it. His balance was suddenly thrown off, and in an instant he hit the magnetic cargo door and was flung out.

When John was thrust out of the plane, the tail lost 185 pounds of cargo, which threw off the dynamics of the flight. The pilot immediately pulled back on the yoke to compensate and yanked it so hard that he knocked out his front teeth. Because of this, the plane stalled. The plane's nose was pointed precariously toward the ground, and the landing was coming forthright.

Neither pilot nor passenger noticed that John was missing. Melanie told me that she realized something wasn't right. "I just started praying," she said. "Something just wasn't right. I hadn't been in a lot of small planes so I didn't really know. It just didn't seem right. I got ready to crash."

The pilot managed to pull off a hard landing on the front wheel with the prop striking the ground. Melanie remembers the right wing was smoking after impact and the tubing was busted on the front tire suspension. She was not hurt, thankfully.

At that point, Melanie turned around to see if John was OK, and that's when she realized he was gone. She ran out of the plane and found him lying on the runway.

With incredible clarity, John recalls the events of that day. He remembers that when he was ejected from his cargo seat, his first thought was, "I can't run that fast." He figures that with the forward motion and speed of the plane, he was probably going around 70 miles per hour. He says the ground was "just coming toward me." He made a conscious decision to get his feet down and start running in the air, since he was at once being propelled forward and down. He hoped this would lessen the impact. He figures he was in the air for about seven seconds before he hit the ground and estimates that he probably fell from a couple hundred feet.

His right foot hit first, and upon impact his heel and half of the sole ripped off his boot. Next his left foot hit, and he flipped over and bounced about 10 to 15 feet in the air, landing headfirst and then spinning around and skidding on his back for a substantial distance before coming to a stop approximately 50 feet beyond the plane.

When Melanie reached him he was trying to get up and looked ashen. She was scared. Their two friends had been standing on the runway and had witnessed the whole thing. They too ran over to offer assistance. That's when John said, "What the hell happened?"

John says he felt no pain. He was in shock. His femur had been broken out of its ball socket at the hip, so as he tried to get up, although the bone was not protruding from the skin, it was pushing against his jeans making a grotesque outline that was evident to Melanie. As he tried to walk, the bone would move 8 inches or so before it would secure itself against his jeans enough to allow him to walk. He said he was putting his hand on the protruding bone and using it as a crutch. He remembers smoke coming from the plane from a wire that had shorted on the battery.

His friends immediately lay him down on the ground. Within minutes he lost sight. He says that at first his vision went to black and white, then it just went dark. He then lost his sense of smell. He wanted to be sure Melanie was there and asked to smell her hand, but he couldn't smell anything and didn't believe it was her when she put her hand to his nose.

Another pilot was summoned and his plane was readied to fly John to Glennallen, where there was a hospital. Once at the hospital, X-rays revealed the broken hip joint and possibly other internal injuries. By this time, John had regained his senses, the loss of which doctors attributed to a concussion he sustained in the fall. A decision was made to transport John to Anchorage by Learjet accompanied by a doctor.

When he finally arrived in Anchorage, John was transported from Merrill Field to the hospital only a couple blocks away by ambulance. He immediately underwent surgery to repair his hip with a plate and a ⅝-inch bolt and, amazingly, that seemed to be his only major injury. While in surgery, the doctors also cleaned up his back, which was pock-marked with gravel and deep abrasions. The impact on the gravel runway had torn through his coat, shirt, T-shirt, and had embedded pea-sized gravel under his skin.

A day or so after surgery, there was still evidence of internal injuries. Doctors also discovered that John was developing gangrene in his back. He underwent surgery again to clean out even more rock, and soon enough his back began to heal. The doctors scheduled exploratory surgery for his internal injuries, but those problems began to clear up on their own in a couple days, so the surgery was canceled.

All in all, John only spent four days in the hospital. They wanted to keep him longer, but when they discovered he didn't have insurance they let him go immediately. He convalesced for four years before he felt back to normal. It also took him four years to pay off the $34,000 bill that resulted.

Asked if he held any ill will against the pilot, he said, "Absolutely not. The flight was as smooth as I've ever had. The pilot didn't do anything wrong. He shouldn't have let me ride in the cargo area, but I shouldn't have accepted either. I just wasn't braced for the banking he made as he approached the runway." The pilot lost his license for four years after the incident, and the plane was considered "wrecked," or totaled.

The incident never prevented John or Melanie from flying in small planes in the future. Now they just make sure they are belted in.

IN HELL AND HIGH WATER

When Mark Freshwaters was a younger man, he spent much of his time in the Alaska wilds making a living as a trapper, using a dog team as transportation.

A hearty and rugged individual, Mark thrived in the backcountry and enjoyed living wild and free. His base of operations was Ruby, on the banks of the Yukon River, but as spring drew closer, he would prepare his gear for a spring camp to hunt for muskrats near the Nowitna River about 30 miles to the east. It was a rush to get his gear, supplies, and dog team to the camp before the warming rays of spring turned trails into slush—presenting a difficult, if not impossible task.

Mark and his dogs had already traveled a significant distance that winter. Mark ran the Iditarod that year and then, after a successful finish, mushed out of Nome with a friend and began the journey back to Ruby. Far from being leisurely, he pushed hard, at times making 100 miles a day in order to return to the village in time to meet Libby, a friend he had invited to join him at his spring camp.

Libby was flown into Mark's trapping cabin and would meet him there. After Mark arrived at the cabin, there was one last push to make it to the spring camp before breakup. They had to cross the Nowitna River and travel a mile or so to reach the camp.

It rained for three days, stalling their progress and making the last leg of the trip a bear. When they finally arrived at their destination, Mark wanted to pick their camping spot carefully. He knew this flat-lying country near the river was prone to flooding.

He saw no evidence of recent flooding, and the pair enjoyed the following couple days of leisurely hunting muskrats and enjoying the warming weather. The lake they were camped on proved a thoroughfare for an ample amount of game, but seemed to be melting before their very eyes.

Trouble was on the horizon.

Because of the rains and quick thaw, the rivers and lakes were overflowing their banks and were beginning to infiltrate the low-lying country surrounding their camp. An ice jam on the Nowitna was forcing large amounts of water into the area, further compromising the assumed safety of the land. Water was beginning to flood their camp.

Planning for the open-water conditions that spring would eventually bring, Mark had enlisted a local pilot to drop his folding canvas kayak at the lake where they were camped. With the rising water, Mark scanned the skies every time a plane flew near, but none dropped his boat. The water was rising as the seconds passed.

With water almost to the top of their hip waders at their camp, Mark and Libby quickly moved to the only spot of higher ground in the area, where they found a large fallen spruce tree wedged between two standing birches. They quickly lashed the sled and their gear to the tree and grabbed some food to eat. Mark had already unhooked his dogs from their chains and the whole lot of them, along with Mark and Libby, huddled on the tiny plot of higher land.

After a dinner of fresh muskrat, they lashed some bedding to the tree, which rested at a 45-degree angle. One person could lie down and rest while the other person stood on the spruce grasping a rope that was tied between the birch trees for support. Meanwhile, water was consuming their little island.

By morning, there was over 4 feet of water below their perch in the tree. The dogs were scrambling for footholds on floating logs and were desperately clinging to whatever they could manage, often falling into the freezing water. Mark hated to see his beloved friends in such a predicament. But there was not much he could do to help them. He says the first night was the hardest, as he worried about the dogs flailing and succumbing to the dark water.

Their second day in the tree, Mark was still holding out hope for the kayak. But Libby was already having second thoughts about the situation. Mark assured her, "You'd be surprised how tough you are. If you had to, I'm sure you could stay up here for four days."

They could have never predicted that their vigil in the tree would last for eight more long and desperate days. Mark would say later, "See, in my wildest dreams I didn't think the water could stay high that long, only receding a few inches every day."

The pair endured cold, listless days stuck up in that tree. They took turns standing and then leaning in the precarious makeshift bed, while their ration of food—scarce from the beginning—dwindled.

On the fifth day, Mark managed to shoot two muskrats that he then retrieved using a lasso with a piece of wood and a treble hook attached. Then he crawled down the tree and started a small fire on one of the floating logs that the dogs were using in order to cook it. Without much wood for a fire, all he managed to do was char the outside, but Mark and Libby ate every inch of the animals. Mark remembers that he even ate the brains, which he called "the best part."

On the sixth day, Mark considered shooting a dog for food. The pair anguished over such a decision. They were shaky and stiff and exhausted from fitful bouts of sleeping while standing up. The sun would sometimes bring them hints of warmth, but not enough to shake the cold that had seeped deep into their bones. They also had to deal with diarrhea. In the worst of times, they occupied themselves with a Louis L'Amour book and a *Reader's Digest* that they had stuffed in their pockets. The dogs were weakening too, and they floundered on the slippery logs, each vying for position on the driest spots. Mark doubted they could hang on much longer.

By the seventh and eighth days, depression had cast a firm shadow over Mark and Libby. It was then that Mark says he seriously wondered if they could last much longer in the tree. Both weak and hypothermic, it was only a matter of time before they wouldn't be able to cling to the tree anymore and would plunge into the icy water. The water was receding, but at such a rate that it seemed it would be several more days, even weeks before they might see the ground again.

The ninth morning brought salvation in the form of wet, mucky earth beneath their tree. The water had completely subsided and they were able to descend for the first time in over a week. During the night, the starving dogs had eaten all the skins from the sled bag that Mark had accumulated from his spring hunting, and although he lost his profits, he was happy his dogs were alive.

When the pair returned to Ruby, they had dinner with friends, who remarked they had never seen anyone eat so much.

Looking back, Mark recalls that those were some pretty wild and rugged times, adding that he "many times pushed [himself] to the limit." And the pilot that was supposed to drop the boat? Well, he delivered it to the wrong lake. The ordeal has forever ruined Mark on muskrat meat.

PASTOR PREACHES PERILS OF BEAR ATTACK

For many years, Pastor Johnny McCoy and Gary Corle of North Pole have enjoyed moose hunting season together in Alaska's backcountry. They would fly out to their favorite area on the Little Delta River and get dropped off for a week or so of hunting—leaving civilization and creature comforts behind. Gary was adamant that the men not have watches or cell phones. He wanted his wilderness uninterrupted and unscheduled.

But the hunt of 2001 would prove to be unlike any they had ever experienced before.

After getting dropped off and setting up camp, the pair got up early the next morning and hiked to their hunting location to scout for moose, about 5 miles away. They both were wearing backpacks and hip waders, and each had their rifles in hand. Johnny had a .300 and Gary had a 30.06. Each gun had a round in the chamber and a round in the magazine.

They slogged through water, brush, and trees, and before long they had nearly reached their destination. That's when things went horribly wrong. At the drop of a dime, a sow came out on the trail and pounced on Gary from behind, knocking him forward into some alders, effectively pinning him in the thick twisted maze of branches. She bit and clawed at his backpack while Gary tried to get his bearings. He was scared she'd get to his head and thought "this is it." But the backpack prevented the bear from reaching his body. He leaned forward for his rifle, and not knowing exactly where the beast was, aimed the gun over his shoulder behind him and poked around until he felt something soft, then pulled the trigger.

Johnny couldn't believe what he was seeing. Gary was just in front of him—maybe 20 yards—during the attack. Johnny had his gun drawn on the bear and wanted to shoot, but if he did he'd hit Gary too. Johnny remembers things happening so fast that he was just trying to figure out what to do.

That's when the bear came at Johnny. Suddenly, she spun around full speed ahead in his direction. At once Johnny brought his gun up and shoved it in her mouth and pulled the trigger—nothing. Again he hit his safety and pulled the trigger—still nothing. The bear hit hard. The momentum of the strike and the weight of his backpack propelled him straight back, and she immediately jumped on his stomach and began tearing into him. She grabbed him by the arms and shook him like a rag doll. The pain was excruciating and Gary could hear Johnny's bones breaking under the force of her vice-grip jaws. Johnny was screaming and trying to protect his face from the beast, which just enraged her all the more.

Gary recalls his friend's screams and says he will never forget the sound. Meanwhile, Gary was trying to extract himself from the alders and get a bead on the bruin with his gun. In such close quarters, all he could see through his scope was a blur of fur. It was a gut-wrenching feeling to watch his friend getting torn apart.

Johnny was now fighting for his life. The bear had moved from his arms to his head and was making mincemeat of his face, teeth scraping against his skull. Essentially scalping him, she bit and clawed at his face, nearly ripping his left ear off and removing an eye from its socket, leaving it dangling down grotesquely on his cheek. The only pain Johnny felt was in his arms. The bear had broken his right arm in nine places and had destroyed his left wrist. Numerous puncture wounds and torn flesh compounded the breaks.

Johnny remembers the intense growling the bear was making throughout the ordeal, as well as the tremendous weight of her upon his stomach and the rancid, rotten-meat smell of her breath.

After what seemed like a lifetime, Johnny just gave up. He stopped screaming and fighting and lay still. He prayed. If the Lord was ready to take him, he was ready to go. He thought of his family and friends and was at peace. The bear stopped tearing at him—her face inches from his—panting and drooling on him. Then, she got off him and walked off, but not before a look back to both of the men. The attack had probably lasted no more than five minutes.

Gary rushed to Johnny's side. Johnny remembers Gary saying, "Pastor, you're in awful shape."

Johnny raised his hand to his face and could feel no pain, as the nerves were demolished. Blood was streaming down his face so he couldn't see. His eyelid and skin were completely ripped off the left side of his face. The wool shirt he was wearing was helping to coagulate the blood from the wounds on his arms, but there was a pencil-sized hole in his left hand squirting blood. Gary grabbed some game bags from his backpack and began to wrap the pastor's wounds as gently and as quickly as possible.

All the while, two bear cubs were in a tree close by and were screaming for their mother. Gary and Johnny knew they had to get out of there fast, but Gary didn't know how they were going to do that.

Luckily, Johnny's torso and lower extremities were unscathed, and with assistance, he was able to stand. Johnny remembers following Gary on the trail—his head and arms heavily wrapped—by touching just his index finger to the back of Gary's pack. Gary led Johnny every step of the way, telling him exactly what kind of terrain they were walking over and how to move. It was 2 miles back to the river, and 3 miles back to camp.

When they reached their camp, Johnny had a surprise for Gary. "Gary," he said, "I've got a cell phone in the tent." Johnny says Gary screamed and hollered with joy. He says he was the happiest man alive.

By now the blood had cleared from Johnny's face and he could see. He could even see out of the eye that was dangling. While Gary retrieved the phone, Johnny sat in a chair. Gary thought he was going to lose his friend. Flustered, Gary asked Johnny who he'd like him to call. Johnny thought that was strange. "Call 911!" he said. Johnny says the phone that he had along was an ancient cell phone—a big one with a large antenna attached. But by the grace of God, they picked up a perfect signal and were able to call for help.

Johnny had previously been the mayor of North Pole and is a widely known figure in the community. The 911 operator knew him and word quickly spread after a call to the church staff and his wife. Within forty-five minutes a rescue helicopter was zooming nearby but couldn't find them. Gary remembers the sinking feeling in his gut as that helicopter came close and then flew out of range. Another guide pilot that was in the area heard the call and knew right where the men were, and he guided the helicopter to them. The chopper landed right in the river and quickly attended to Johnny's wounds before lifting off for Fairbanks Memorial Hospital. Johnny always said he wanted to ride in a helicopter and was now getting his wish.

Within twenty minutes he was at the hospital, the helicopter landing at the same time as his wife arrived. He was met at the door by a team of doctors in the ER, many of whom he knew, who began to cut his clothes off. "Please don't cut my hip waders off—they're $200 boots!" he said. And to Johnny's relief, they obliged. Johnny remembers lots of whispering between the doctors, and he was constantly telling them, "Don't whisper—I want to know what's going on!" He says he was hungry and had to go to the bathroom. But he was headed straight for surgery. Luckily, a plastic surgeon was on the floor that day, as well as another skilled doctor who had handled lots of bear attacks in the past. He says Johnny's was the worst he had ever seen.

After six hours of surgery, Johnny came out all pieced back together—his head laced with over 1,500 tiny stitches—his arms 200 and 150, respectively. With tubes coming out everywhere, he was put in intensive care.

The doctors were initially concerned about his ear taking, as it was turning black, but it ended up healing fine. His eye sustained not a trace of damage and was refitted in its socket. Johnny now says that eye has better vision than his other one. His skin had been retrieved from the game bags that initially wrapped his face and was reattached to his scalp, including the eyelashes from his left eye.

Two days after the attack, Johnny got brave enough to look in the mirror: "I thought, 'Geez, someone hit you with an ugly stick!'" Within two weeks he was back to get the stitches out, which he says was very painful. Since it was a plastic surgeon that fixed him up, each stitch was minute and painstakingly placed. Johnny has never needed any facial plastic surgery due directly to that plastic surgeon's finesse with a needle. If you saw Johnny today, you would never know he had been a victim of a vicious bear attack.

Within weeks Johnny was back at the pulpit with a heartfelt message and renewed spirit. God had spared his life, and to him Johnny gave all the glory. Johnny's arms were in casts for a long time, and it took over a year for him to completely heal. The only lasting physical effect is a weak grip in his left hand.

A year after the mauling, Johnny, Gary, and Johnny's son returned to the site. As they were walking near the area, Johnny's son found the bolt and cartridges for Johnny's rifle. Apparently they had fallen out and that was why his shot never found its mark in the bear's mouth. They also discovered the remains of the bear—just the skull and a few scattered bones. He regrets the bear cubs that probably died, as well as the death of the mother bear. "She was just doing what came naturally to her—protecting her cubs," he says.

Johnny has had the opportunity to speak to thousands of people about his experience. He has received letters and phone calls from around the world and frequently makes trips to other states and countries to tell his story—always with a message of God's grace. His story even appeared on *Outdoor Life*'s "This Happened to Me" television segment, in which the incident was reenacted. Johnny will never forget what that bear looked like, what she smelled like—the growling and the way she sat on him. He says she pounced faster than any cat he's ever seen. Johnny is just thankful to be alive, and grateful for the chance to tell his story.

11

Extremely Alaskan: Sports on the Edge

Here in Alaska we take everything to extremes—including our sports. Take for instance Arctic Man. This event pairs downhill skiers and snowmachiners in a test of wills against gravity and sanity as skiers reach speeds upward of 80 miles per hour while careening down a remote mountain toward the finish line. Or how about the Pillar Mountain Golf Classic in Kodiak—a par 70, one-hole winter golf tournament that ascends a 1,400-foot peak? Whether these types of sports chance all or nothing, they all say at once: Alaskans are tough. Here's a salute to some of the wildest races and competitors out there.

MOUNT MARATHON

Fun Facts

Where: Seward

When: July 4

What: Mad-dash footrace

Length: 3 miles (1½ up, 1½ down)

Elevation: 3,022 feet

Slope: 45 degrees

Terrain: Mud, dirt, loose shale, rock, waterfalls, snow

Entry fee: $35 adults, $20 juniors

Special auction: If the race is full, you can bid on ten spots that are auctioned off for the men's and women's races the night before. Most go for around $400 to $600 dollars, with a very high bid being around $900.

>>

Competitors: 350 men, 350 women, open Juniors Race (seventeen and under)
Prizes: You get a T-shirt and patch when you finish. What do winners get? A T-shirt and a patch.
Information: 907-224-8051, *visitseward@seward.net,* *www.sewardak.org*

My own taste of extreme adventure began with a plastic toilet seat at 10 below during my first Alaskan winter. After that, I naturally decided I wanted to try the Mount Marathon foot race in Seward. Of course the only thing these two events have in common is the ability to propel grown people into sad displays of mama begging.

I'd heard about this race for years. It was legendary. Seems two old sourdoughs were arguing one day over drinks as to whether or not a person could climb and descend the mountain in an hour or less. Bets were placed and a race was on. The winner crossed the line in an hour and two minutes, and since 1915 an official race has been run on the mountain every Fourth of July.

I was a happy, healthy, and very large pregnant woman when I decided I wanted to run the race. If all went well, I would give birth and three months later be at the starting line of one Alaska's most famous extreme races. This is just another example of why pregnant women should not be allowed to make their own decisions.

Of course I had to get the golden ticket first. This race is so popular that you can't just show up on race day and expect a bib number. Unless you ran the previous year's race, or are a veteran of ten races or more in your lifetime, you have to apply for a lottery drawing to glean a toe on the starting line. My award letter came in the mail in March, and I was officially screwed—I mean invited to the race!

I was feeling less optimistic about my racing instincts after I had my son. Long sleepless nights, leaking boobs, and my overactive two-year-old were getting the best of me. But I trained hard and found myself in some kind of shape come July. Not good shape, just some kind of shape. After all, running on gym treadmills twice a week really *can* simulate the most rigorous of outdoor environs!

After a quick plane ride to Anchorage from Fairbanks and then an enjoyable ride on one of Alaska's busiest highways on the Fourth of July weekend, I arrived in Seward for a look-see. There were people everywhere. I mean everywhere. I've never seen anything like it except for on TV in Times Square on New Year's Eve. I had planned on camping out somewhere but knew that I was going to have to travel a good distance out of town even to find a spot to park my compact rental car.

The prerace meeting required for new racers was enlightening. Essentially, it was a video littered with language like "extremely dangerous," "EMT's will be standing by," and "it's not too late to save yourself." It showed weary racers puking off the side of the trail and bloodied humans (?) flailing down the steep scree slope, some on their butts and some on their heads trying to "get a better time."

I stood in line defiantly unfazed to receive my bib number and then raced to the bathroom to pump my breasts.

That night I packed myself into the back seat of my rental car at a lake about 20 miles outside of Seward. It was peaceful away from all the crowds and madness of the holiday weekend. I had time to relax in that back seat and just knew that the race would turn out all right.

Next morning, I awoke early in a fetal position and began my nutritional preparations for the day. I once again had to pump my breasts, as I had been doing almost every two hours since arriving. But this got me thinking. Breast milk was supposed to be so good for you—well, for your baby—packed full of nutrients and stuff. Maybe it had qualities that my energy drinks lacked. I looked at the 4-ounce bottle and thought, "What the heck," and gulped it with my nose plugged. Then I ate an energy bar and did some jumping jacks around the parking lot.

A couple hours before race time, I made my way back to Seward so I could find a parking spot within 5 miles of the starting line. I was feeling good, though jittery and a little like I had to use the bathroom. There were hordes of people

TIPS FOR GETTING INTO RACE SHAPE— ALASKA STYLE

For Strength:

• Find two trees. Cut, split, and stack in nice rows. Burn in woodstove. Repeat when cold (next day).

• Go fishing. Catch a 400-pound halibut and play it for five hours.

• Hook yourself up to a dogsled and take your kids for a ride.

• Steer your vehicle violently into a ditch. Carry a snow shovel with you.

• Arm-wrestle the average Alaskan woman.

already watching the Junior Race in progress, and seeing the excitement really made me have to go. But this was no ordinary feeling, it felt like something more like diarrhea. I raced to the Porta Potti in time to confirm my fears. It was then I realized how babies can handle breast milk: they wear diapers.

MOUNT MARATHON ADVICE FROM A SAGE COMPETITOR (NOT ME)

- Train, train, train. Climb stairs or hills for more than an hour more than twice a week. While running. With a pack on. While on fire.

- Don't try "break through" energy drinks the day of the race. Trust me.

- You might have more fun if you wear a chicken suit.

- There may or may not be water available on the mountain. Maybe.

When it was time, I lined up with all the other women racing and before I knew it I was out of breath and wishing I were home. Then the gun went off. The horde of us raced the ½ mile to the base of the mountain and then began our goat climb to the 3,022-foot peak. I felt like a rock star with all the people cheering us on along the streets, but soon enough, I think death by lethal injection would have been more enjoyable. The going was so steep and rugged that you could literally only follow in the footsteps of the person one second in front of you. There was no passing on the single-track trail. I had to stop twice early on and get off the trail to halt the overwhelming urge to vomit.

After a while, though, I finally found my rhythm, and as I got above the trees and scrub brush on the mountain and could see views of the town, ocean, and immense scenery, my mood started to lighten. It was no longer a race. It was an experience.

I was told there would be water at the top, and other racers had said there might be water halfway up the mountain too. Neither proved true, and I hadn't brought any water with me. So I was delighted by the little sips of water on offer from the hearty souls who had climbed up to cheer the racers and were handing over their own water bottles.

I also got to take pictures as I went along. I had cut the top part of an old tube sock to use as an armband in which to carry a disposable camera with me. I got some excellent pictures, and I had even more fun along the way. Although one lady was a little bitter when I took her picture. I told her I was taking pictures of all the slow people as I passed them and that she should find me after the race and give me her e-mail. I guess she wasn't in the mood to talk.

Once I reached the top, I had the race officials take my picture and then was relieved to begin the downhill portion. All of a sudden, rubber legs were expected to keep downhill momentum in check, which was all but impossible. The slope was covered in marble-sized pieces of shale and free-flowing dirt, which might as well have been a landslide. I made giant leaps in the air and all this material would just slide down with each landing to cushion the blow. You could really fly and I was having quite a time of it—smiling real big and bantering with any spectators along the mountain as I leapt by. It was much like running down a giant sand dune—except that sand is soft. If you fell in this stuff it would cut you to ribbons and probably roll you all the way to Florida.

The other problem I was having was that my shoes were getting stuffed full of this rock and dirt, making it feel like I was running on glass when I finally reached the street in the final part of the race. I had to sit down and empty out one shoe, as I just couldn't take it anymore. Besides that, I had only one small cut on a finger from a razor-sharp shale section near the bottom. I managed to cross the finish line backward as I took a picture of myself.

I collapsed in a heap on a curb and drank a pint of water with my shoes off. Running the race left me with a satisfying feeling, yet one that I don't care to repeat anytime soon. Probably one of those "once in a lifetime" things. On the other hand, I would like to see if I could do better with someone else's body.

- For fun, if a large rock is heading downslope don't yell, "Rock!" Yell, "I'm thirsty!"

- The race will begin without you, so be late if you'd like.

- All the prerace hysteria is just hype. Only 30 percent of competitors die.

- The mountain really isn't that steep once you get crawling.

- The town shows up for the wrecks, not the race. Blood is cool.

- Don't eat burritos at the street fair before the race.

I finished in the middle of the pack, while the winner finished in under an hour. I suspect she didn't have a breast milk energy drink before the race or carry a camera in a tube sock on her arm.

The good news is I got a shower after the race, and my body shut down any need to pump my breasts for days to come. And so it was for the diarrhea too. I couldn't walk right for days after and it hurt to breathe, but I would say overall the race was a success.

IDITAROD TRAIL INVITATIONAL

The world's longest, human-powered winter ultra-marathon.

Fast Facts

Where: Knik Lake to McGrath

When: Third week of February

What: Human-powered adventure race

Length: 350 miles

Mode of travel: Bike, skis, or feet

Entry fee: $700, includes some food and lodging along the trail and two food drops

Prizes: T-shirt and poster

Bonus: Some racers keep going all the way to Nome, 1,049 miles, which is the official finish for the Iditarod sled dog race

Course records: Bike—Mike Curiak, 2005, 3 days, 6 hours; Skis— Jim Jeager, 2002, 4 days, 8 hours; Feet—Steve Reifenstuhl, 2005, 4 days, 15 hours

Information: Race Director Bill Merchant at 907-775-1533, *billmerchant@alaskaultrasport.com, www.alaskaultrasport.com*

A human-powered adventure race, the Iditarod Trail Invitational is indeed an adventure. As with other events in this chapter, you have to be just a little bit nuts to bike, walk, or ski the 350 desolate miles across Alaska that defines the race. Starting at Knik Lake and ending in McGrath, the race follows the Iditarod trail, where racers are submitted to the law of extremes. Temperatures can plummet, you can lose the trail, your water can freeze, you can run out of food, your gear can break, weather can come in, and the list goes on. One racer called it a "suffer-fest." Another dubbed it "the Yukon death march." With those kinds of descriptions, who wouldn't want to race?

There are seven checkpoints where racers can get some food and rest, but between checkpoints racers are on their own. Distances between checkpoints range from 30 to 75 miles. There are no support crews, and you can take any route you'd like as long as you check in and out of the mandatory checkpoints.

Many decide to travel as light and fast as possible, carrying bare minimums in terms of food and gear to get by until they reach each checkpoint. There are also two food drops allowed, which can weigh no more than 10 pounds each. This can help racers resupply when needed.

Those who haven't taken enough of a beating can continue on for another 699 miles to Nome without support and be met at the finish line by no one.

ARCTIC MAN SKI AND SNO GO CLASSIC

Go fast, or go home.

Fast Facts

Where: Hoodoo Mountains near Summit Lake, just north of Paxson

When: April

What: Teams of one snowmachiner and one skier alternate towing and skiing at breakneck speeds up and down sections of a remote mountain in a race to the finish line

Highest point: 5,800 feet

Finish line: 2,900 feet

Entry fee: $900

Prizes: Cash purse

Competitors: 50 men and women's teams, 30 men and women's snowboard teams

Record: Skier Eric Heil and snowmachiner Len Story in 2005—89.3 miles per hour, finish time of 4:04.33

Information: 907-456-2626, *arcticmn@alaska.net,* *www.arcticman.com*

At the ultra-insane Arctic Man Ski and Sno Go Classic, skiers and snowmachine riders are paired in an event unlike any other. The skier starts at an elevation of 5,800 feet and skis down 1,700 feet in less than 2 miles to meet his riding partner. There, they pair up on the fly and the snowmachiner pulls the skier using a tow rope up a 2¼ mile rise approaching speeds of 80 miles per hour. Then, the skier drops the tow rope and speeds down the final 1,200 feet to the finish line. It takes a whole lotta crazy to ride this train.

Howard Thies, founder and organizer of this phenomenon, skied the area himself when he was younger and the whole idea of pairing a snowmachiner and a skier began as a challenge from friends in 1986. It's been an annual event since then.

This fast and frenzied race course attracts and delights from twelve to thirteen thousand people annually at Summit Lake, the event's home. There is no town—not a hotel room for hundreds of miles, save for an old lodge and a few cabins here and there. Snow plows clear rows and rows of RV parking in the vast, flat staging grounds at the base of the Hoodoo Mountains—the playground for Arctic Man. For that week in April, the crowds equal something like the fourth largest city in Alaska. Bonfires, lawn chairs, and Porta Pottis abound. The beer tent provides an obvious attraction, but besides that hosts nightly entertainment and information about the racing.

In 2005, the twentieth anniversary of the event, Warren Miller of extreme ski movie fame filmed the happenings. A six-minute cut of Arctic Man appeared in his *Higher Ground* movie and was well received, giving Howard Thies hope for more participants in an already exciting field (visit the filmmaker's website to purchase the DVD, *www.warrenmiller.com*).

TIPS FOR GETTING INTO RACE SHAPE— ALASKA STYLE

For Agility:

- **Find two trees on someone else's property. Cut them down. Now run.**

- **Try ice skating on the Bering Sea.**

- **Run when you see a bear.**

- **Learn the Eskimo roll in a kayak.**

- **Catch a 400-pound halibut. Once it's on board, let it flop around violently while you jump around to save your life.**

TESORO IRON DOG

The longest, toughest snowmobile race in the world.

Fast Facts

Where: Wasilla to Nome to Fairbanks

When: February

What: Snowmachine race

Length: 1,851 miles in 2006

Entry fees: Trail (recreational) class, $2,560; pro class, $4,060; fees per team of two

Prizes: Sliding-scale payout based on number of finishers; purse for 2005 was $75,000 split among top six teams—winning team took home $23,250

Information: 907-563-4414, *info@irondog.org, www.irondog.org*

I don't know much about riding snowmachines, but an 1,800-mile trip across some of Alaska's wildest country on one does not sound like a walk in the park. Considering what the racers face, this race is indeed a test of human and machine endurance.

Two people comprise a team, and all riders must follow strict rules about snowmachine modifications. Weather conditions can sabotage even the most well-laid plan. Blowing and drifting snow and ground blizzards can obscure the trail, creating the very real possibility of racers getting lost at any moment. There is also the reality of bitterly cold temperatures and wind chills that can freeze snowmachines and men in their tracks. Open water is yet another obstacle. River travel is common, as is the necessary travel across the Bering Sea, where ice ridges and rotten ice can literally sink a team.

Racers are, by necessity, mechanics, and they must fix their machines along the trail at any point in order to keep them going. Breakdowns are a major part of the race. One lead racer has been said to have rebuilt his engine three times on the trail before he broke down for the fourth time and finally ran out of parts. Racers are required to have at least 5 pounds of tools with them.

Trail conditions, or the lack thereof, also give racers considerable pause. Early leaders can really tear up the trail on steep inclines or in questionable areas, leaving racers that follow to pick up the pieces of a hole-pocked, hell-bent, snowmachine-swallowing trail. Over half the teams that enter the race will scratch for one reason or another. But those who endure the fifty to sixty hours of pounding trail, the dicey weather conditions, and the mental strains can boast of conquering the Iron Dog.

PILLAR MOUNTAIN GOLF CLASSIC

Fast Facts

Where: Kodiak Island

When: March

What: One-hole, par 70 romp up Pillar Mountain

Hazards: Bears, snow, alder thickets

Entry fee: $50 donation

Prizes: Cash and awards

Information: Tony's Bar (unofficial clubhouse) at 907-486-9489, *wkoning@ptialaska.net, www.chiniak.net/pillar*

Golfing in Alaska is a lesson in survival. Due to widely varying weather conditions, 4x4 terrain, and the bonus threat of predatory carnivores, golfers are not allowed to wear preppy shirts or whine. You may, though, shoulder a sidearm if you choose.

Bears are probably one of first things that come to mind when people think of Alaska. Bears on a golf course though—probably not. But on Kodiak Island, home of the giant Kodiak brown bear, you'd be wise to heed the scorecard advice from the Pillar Mountain Golf Classic: "Don't wake up the bears. (Five stroke penalty...)."

This one-hole, par 70 par golf course is a challenge in itself, even without those pesky spring bears. Every March, golfers pay an entry fee, enlist the help of a spotter and a caddy, and then take on the 1,400-foot Pillar Mountain in a quest to drive their golf ball up the mountain to a 5-gallon bucket hole buried in snow at the top.

Golfers are advised to bring brush-cutting equipment for the rough (alders), but no chain saws are allowed. Cursing the officials will cost you $25. Litterbugs will be eliminated. All you have to do is get your ball to the top of the mountain. Easy as that.

The Pillar Mountain Golf Classic has been in place since 1984 and is put on by the Professional Cross Country Golfer's Association, a local nonprofit. Proceeds support local charities.

BERING SEA ICE GOLF CLASSIC

Fast Facts

Where: Bering Sea, off the coast of Nome
When: Third Saturday in March
What: Par 41 course on sea ice
Hazards: Polar bears, cracks in ice
Entry fee: $50
Prizes: T-shirt, small bottles of liquor, and certificate
Information: 907-443-6624, *tourinfo@ci.nome.ak.us*, *www.nomealaska.org/vc/festivals.htm*

Playing on the frozen six-hole, par 41 golf course on the Bering Sea coast of Nome would certainly qualify as one of those "only in Alaska" experiences. Add a guy in a Santa suit with a canopy-covered snowmachine "golf cart" and a caddy dressed up like a chicken—well that's just friggin' funny (dressing in costume is encouraged).

You have to love the spirit of the folks who play this annual course, where the rough might include slushy ice or pressure ridges and the green is fake patio grass around a sunken coffee-can hole with a bright flag sticking out of it. Other hazards include polar bears—the scorecard says if you hit one with your ball, you have to add three strokes to your score. No swimming in the water hazards is allowed (dang it!). Spent shotgun shells are used as tees and should not be left behind.

If you gotta have the T-shirt (and the two tiny complimentary bottles of liquor provided at the start), you'd better sign up for next year's tournament. With all the global warming we're experiencing, there may not be an Ice Golf Classic in a few years. And that T-shirt will be worth a mint on eBay.

FARTHEST NORTH FOREST SPORTS FESTIVAL

All-star gathering of sharp tools and dull wits.

Fast Facts

Where: University of Alaska-Fairbanks experimental farm field below the railroad tracks, Fairbanks

When: October

What: Lumberjack skills contests

Who: Open to the public

Judges: UAF Department of Forest Sciences professors

Prizes: If you keep your fingers, you've won.

Information: *http://nrm.salrm.uaf.edu/~jfox/ForSciDept/ForestSportsBlurb.html*

Have you got a hankering to see how good you can throw an ax? How 'bout showing off your log bucking talent? Well, for one glorious day in Fairbanks, you can flash those bona fide logging skills in a match of man (or woman) against wood. Or at least you can wear some Carhartts and a flannel and look cool.

Sponsored annually by the University of Alaska–Fairbanks Department of Forest Sciences, this festival includes all the classic lumberjack event categories: men and women's double-buck, men and women's single-buck, Jack and Jill double-buck, ax throw, log roll, fire building, pulp toss, and birling. (If you're already lost, you better stick to Monopoly.)

Logging skills never go out of style in Alaska and may well prove to be a great tool in obtaining a mate. If you prefer your guy or girl to be the rugged, Carhartt-wearing kind, you'll find yourself in good company here.

The big finale of the day is the Carhartt and Flannel Ball, put on by the Alaska Boreal Forest Council. The ball comes complete with music, appetizers, dancing, a silent auction, prizes for best dressed and is *the* best place to find the Carhartt man or woman of your dreams. Visit the council's website for more information (*www.akborealforest.org*).

THE YUKON QUEST

The toughest sled dog race in the world.

Fast Facts

Where: Fairbanks, Alaska, to Whitehorse, Yukon, Canada (direction switches every year)

When: February

What: Sled dog race

Length: 1,000 miles, ten to thirteen days to finish

Dog minimums/maximums: Must start with no more than fourteen, end with no less than six

Layover: One thirty-six hour layover required in Dawson City

Entry fee: $1,250

Prizes: Top fifteen finishers split $125,000, with the winner taking home $30,000

Special prize: Last musher in receives the Red Lantern Award and takes home...a red lantern.

Course record: Frank Turner of Whitehorse in 1995—10 days, 16 hours, 20 minutes

Information: 907-452-7954, *yukonquest@mosquitonet.com*, *www.yukonquest.org*

You've probably heard of the Iditarod, but the Yukon Quest is the real test of endurance for qualified sled dog racers. It's said to be tougher, more remote, and without all the glory of the Iditarod. Mushers start the race in Fairbanks or Whitehorse, depending on the year, and travel 1,000 miles over some of the wildest country North America has to offer.

The logistics of the race alone would make most people think twice about entering. The mushers and their dogs are out on the trail anywhere from ten to sixteen days. Food drops ensure that each musher will have the food and supplies needed to see them through the race. This takes an incredible amount of planning. During the race handlers can only physically help the musher at the layover in Dawson City. Otherwise, the musher must handle all the feeding and care of their dogs, as well as repair the sled or any broken gear as it occurs. Only after the dogs are cared for can mushers take care of themselves, and many go for days with little to no sleep. The dogs are inspected at every checkpoint in order to keep them healthy.

Harsh conditions plague many teams along the way. Since the race is held in the heart of winter, the weather is wildly unpredictable. Temperatures as low as 40 below have been recorded, as have temperatures of 25 degrees Fahrenheit. Mushers may encounter overflow conditions, windswept trails, steep terrain, exposed rocks, and/or open water. Add to that the threat of running into a moose and getting your team stomped or falling asleep on the runners and waking up with a bloody mouth from a branch that hit you in the face.

Although the Yukon Quest doesn't have the Iditarod's notoriety, its fiercely loyal fans in Canada and Alaska believe this is the race to end all sled dog races. And I think the mushers and dogs would agree.

YUKON 800

The longest, roughest, toughest speed boat race in the world.

Fast Facts

Where: Chena, Tanana, and Yukon Rivers, from Fairbanks to Galena and back

When: June

What: Boat race with ultrasleek handmade river boats

Length: 800 miles

Entry fee: $20 membership to Fairbanks Outboard Association plus variable race entry fee

Course record: Harold Attla in 2001—11 hours, 54 minutes, 9 seconds

Information: *www.yukon800.com*

The Doyon Limited Yukon 800 boat race is a sight to see. Of course, you'll only get to witness a few seconds of the race at a time, but it still proves to be a fun race to follow. Riding ultrasleek handmade race boats of 24 feet or longer, a captain and a team consisting of an engineer and a navigator travel first the Chena, then the Tanana, and finally the Yukon River along a watery race course that leads them to Galena for an overnight layover, and then back to Fairbanks in the morning for the finish.

This is not your average boat ride. The boats are designed with speed in mind, streamlined and built from a framework of Sitka spruce and with a hull of ¼- or ⅛-inch plywood. Each team's low-slung boat is a lesson in aerodynamics and runs so fast that at times they seem to just barely skim the water. Crew members sometimes fight to keep the bow down and splay their bodies across the boat to keep it under control. Powered by regulation 50-horsepower motors, boats routinely hit the 70-mile-per-hour mark along the course.

But dangers lurk just beneath the surface. The boaters must be ultra-aware of the hazards that can at best slow them down, or at worse cause an accident. Floating logs and debris, hidden sand or gravel bars, and submerged sweepers can wreak havoc on a boat's hull and motor. Then there are meteorological conditions to worry about: fog, windblown sand, rain, and hail, smoke from wildfires, or high winds can all upend even the most seasoned crews. Add to that the water conditions. Flat water can make you feel like you're "driving on pavement," as one racer put it. But upstream winds can create large waves, which led one racer to comment, "I felt like I just went twelve rounds with the heavyweight champion."

The rooster tails are the signal to watch for as the racers round the bend to the finish line. It may not be the best spectator sport, but for the racers, the Yukon 800 is all about having fun and beating the odds.

TIPS FOR GETTING INTO RACE SHAPE— ALASKA STYLE

For Endurance:

- **Watch one day less of TV every week all winter.**

- **Play Monopoly.**

- **Lock yourself in a cabin with your mate for the entire month of January. No booze allowed.**

- **Remember the cigarettes, but forget the matches.**

- **Let your snowmachine run out of gas in the wilderness.**

RED GREEN RIVER REGATTA

Fast Facts

Where: Chena River, Fairbanks

When: July

What: A homemade-boat race using at least one roll of duct tape

Prizes: Locally-donated prizes for the top three finalists

Information: 907-474-7491, *events@alaskaone.org*, *www.alaskaone.org*

Every July, throngs of dedicated admirers of Canada's original duct tape aficionado, Red Green, honor the icon by hosting a boat race in the spirit of his popular TV series, *The Red Green Show.* In the show, Green uses duct tape to construct, fix, and invent ingenious and handy objects. Racers don't have many rules to follow. Their boats must be made from at least one roll of duct tape, show creativity in using a Red Green attitude for construction, and be able to stay afloat. Judges determine the winner of this "nonrace" based on originality and the above mentioned points, not who crosses the finish line first.

CHATANIKA OUTHOUSE RACES

Fast Facts

Where: Chatanika Lodge, 28 miles north of Fairbanks on the Steese Highway

When: March

What: Chatanika Days

Information: 907-389-2164

When it comes to extremes, Alaskans take the cake for riding the extreme side of just about everything—and that includes our normal, everyday off time. Chalk it up to too much sun or too much darkness, or all that liquor—ask anyone and they'll likely agree that we're just a little bit kooky. A good time to us is rigging up an outhouse and racing the sucker around a 1-mile track in the snow. We don't mess around, see, when it comes to having a good time.

On the outhouse-racing circuit, this one's the champ. Here you will find genuine backwoods mentality mixed with just the right amount of libations to provide an entertaining show for all. Teams are comprised of four "pushers" and one "in the hole." The track is a dangerously curvy 1-mile loop that's flanked by an extremely boisterous crowd. Well, OK, the track is pretty straight and mild, but the crowd can be dangerous. You have to build your outhouse racer—no showroom models allowed.

THE SLUSH CUP

Fast Facts

Where: Alyeska Resort, Girdwood
When: April
What: Spring Carnival
Information: 907-754-2108, *guestservices@alyeskaresort.com,*
www.alyeskaresort.com

Every year, Alyeska Resort in Girdwood kicks winter in the butt with their annual Spring Carnival and Slush Cup—the symbolic start of the green season. In the Slush Cup the object is to dress as funky as possible, strap on some skis or a snowboard, and careen down a hill at the speed of sound toward a man-made pond full of icy water that the skier must then glide across, or face-plant in—as most likely results—to the applause and deafening cheers of the sometimes inebriated, boisterous crowd behind the ski fence. The winner is determined by air time, costume, crowd response, and style.

POLAR BEAR JUMP-OFF FESTIVAL

Fast Facts

Where: Seward

When: January

What: Crazy, costumed folks jumping into Resurrection Bay in the dead of winter

Information: 907-224-8051, *visitseward@seward.net*, *www.sewardak.org*

At a chilly 35 degrees Fahrenheit, you wouldn't think people would be lining up for a chance to take a swim in the frigid water of Resurrection Bay in Seward. But they do. Year after year, since 1986, the Polar Bear Jump-off Festival has garnered attention as "the thing to do" if you're in the vicinity of Seward round about the balmy month of January. These people may be a bit crazy, but they're also raising money for charities—the name of the game. It's also a lot of fun to dress up as the Hamburglar or Elvis or a chicken before jumping into the icy water. Yep, costumes are required, at least if you really want to have some fun.

MOUNTAIN MOTHER CONTEST

Fast Facts

Where: Talkeetna

When: July

What: A timed obstacle course of mountain motherly skills

Prizes: Mountain Mother Champion jacket for the winner; gift baskets for the top three finishers

Information: 907-733-2330, *www.talkeetnachamber.org*

Crossing logs with waders on, hauling water and groceries, chopping wood, catching fish, shooting a bow, pounding nails, making dinner, hanging out laundry—yes, we women in Alaska do these things every day. Oh, and our babies are never far from our backpacks. That essentially is the Mountain Mother Contest in a nutshell—a timed event that showcases the skills of the mountain mother with hip waders on and a "baby" in a backpack.

12

Wilderness Travel and Other Misguided Adventures for Your Personal Enjoyment

Alaska is an outdoor lover's paradise. That's why most people live here—to enjoy the vast natural resources at their fingertips. There are a lot of choices for where to travel and what to do, and it would take most of a lifetime just to skim the surface of the places to see. Some of my best memories have been while out frolicking in Alaska's playground. From quirky roadside stops with cereal-box collections, to relationship-ending river travel, to life-threatening wilderness encounters with porcupines, there's no place I'd rather be.

BEARS, PORCUPINES, AND GUNS THAT WORK GREAT AT NIGHT

Adventuring in Alaska is dangerous. As a former guide for various activities around the state, I've had my share of scary moments. I've seen an elderly man flip an ATV onto himself. I've deposited two Japanese tourists out of a raft into freezing waters—shouting what to do at them in English while they only spoke their native tongue. I've had to rescue tipped canoeists and have had to attend to a tourist who broke her leg while dog mushing. I've been followed by a bear and have burned up my boots in a campfire miles from the trailhead (long story). I'm sure there are more, but those are the ones I can remember off the top of my head.

But that's what makes this state so great! The adventures are genuine, heart-thumping, and sometimes life-threatening. But when all is said and done, you will find yourself with a renewed spirit and a thirst for life unlike anything you will probably ever experience (if you don't die, that is). Wilderness travel is just like that.

One of my most favorite jobs was a gig as a fishing guide/cook aboard a 30-by 70-foot log raft on the Yukon River. The raft served as the base camp, and I got to take people out in a skiff to fish the tributaries for pike, sheefish, and grayling. I was also in charge of cooking and navigating the raft when necessary. It was the summer of my dreams. For weeks on end we lazily floated down the majestic Yukon in search of big fish, fantastic scenery, and a quiet like you wouldn't believe. Most of the guests went away with the trip of a lifetime.

One morning, just after the guests had left the night before, I was awakened by the sound of claws walking across the plank flooring of the raft. We were tied up to shore as usual, so my first thought was, "It's a bear!" As the claws made their way around the raft, I grabbed my gun and tried to determine how I was going to wake up my boss and the other guide who were sound asleep in another tent without getting killed by the predator that was freely roaming the raft. I could see nothing out of the small back window in my canvas wall tent, which faced the woods. The only way I could get a look at what was out there was if I got down on the floor and peeked out from under the front of my tent. I didn't want to chance opening my zipper without knowing where the beast was (I knew I was perfectly safe behind that 12-ounce waterproof duck canvas).

The sound stopped. Had it heard me getting my gun? Where was it now? I was now lying prone, eyeballs one inch from the bottom of my tent, ready to peek out. More silence. I had to look out there. I slowly lifted the tent to accommodate just my nose and eyeballs, and there it was! I was face to face with a porcupine.

I breathed a sigh of relief and gently nudged the "beast" off the raft with a shovel.

For a tough outdoors girl, I must admit I'm not fond of the dark. So when I was left alone on the raft for the span of a week, I had to manage my fears knowing I was basically sleeping on a curious island of good-smelling food and was awash in human blood ready for the taking. With the previous week's porcupine experience, I knew it was entirely possible that other things might come to check out the raft. So on the first night, I was prepared.

I searched the raft and found anything I could stack—beer and soda cans, cans of bug spray, and cans of vegetables (that was a wise choice)—and booby-trapped all the entrance points to the raft from shore. If anything was going to come on the raft with foul intentions, I figured it would knock over all the stuff, wake me up, and give me time to access one of the three rifles or the grenade launcher that was waiting under my cot.

Unfortunately, I never got to see my plan executed. The only thing that resulted was an incredible hangover from a lack of sleep. I did prove to myself that I am woman enough to endure a week alone in the wilderness on a really nice raft complete with comfortable cot, food, and the necessary fire power.

But dang it, I'm still afraid of the dark.

THE RIVER TRIP TO END ALL RIVER TRIPS

Adventuring by river is a very enjoyable way to see the state. You can carry more gear than you could backpacking (like a Coleman stove, a stove-top espresso maker, and extra chocolate), making your wilderness journey a real treat. Although there is always the threat of capsizing, that's what keeps things interesting. River travel is by far my favorite way to experience Alaska. For a memorable trip, nothing beats the Yukon.

A Yukon River Float

The fabled 2,000-mile Yukon River has a rich history in both Canada and Alaska, starting with the Native peoples who used (and still use) the river for hunting and fishing, then with expeditions and fur trading, and finally with the gold rushes of the late nineteenth and early twentieth centuries bringing stampeders and, later, stern-wheelers up and down the river. As such, the river offers paddlers both a historic and cultural glance along their wilderness journey.

The whole length of the silty, caramel-colored Yukon can be floated with proper planning, and the adventures of those willing to devote their entire summer to this end have been chronicled in many books. A paddler looking for a road-accessible entry and exit has the following options:

- Whitehorse, Yukon, to Dawson City, Yukon (468 miles, 10–16 days)
- Dawson City, Yukon, to Eagle, Alaska (104 miles, 2–5 days)
- Eagle, Alaska, to Circle City, Alaska (151 miles, 3–7 days)
- Circle City, Alaska, to the Haul Road Bridge on the Dalton Highway, Alaska (257 miles, 7–14 days)

The placid river is easy to navigate and any number of craft can successfully float the river. Canoes are by far the most popular.

The Yukon is a constantly changing body of water with various currents, channels, and hidden sandbars. Because of the vast wilderness, the Yukon can be a lonely place, with help many miles away. Make sure to brush up on your boating skills, your survival skills, and basic first aid. Common sense will be your biggest ally. Leave plenty of room in your itinerary for an extra day here and there. Always wear a life jacket and avoid traveling alone.

Consult local maps and charts for the section of river you will be traveling, and make sure to leave your travel plans with a friend. Also, be prepared to deal with the bugs. Camping is available on sandbars and along the banks of the river. Wild animals are prevalent, so keeping a clean camp is imperative.

Most of the villages along the river offer basic services, such as a grocery store, post office, gas, phone, laundry, and shower facilities. But expect to pay a bit more in these remote locations. Lodging is scarce, but may be found simply by asking around. Generally, there are bush flights to and from these villages daily, but it would be wise to check into it before you end up stranded.

An excellent guide on floating the Yukon River is Dan Maclean's *Paddling the Yukon River and its Tributaries.*

Canoes can be rented for the Whitehorse, Dawson City, Eagle, or Circle City sections by contacting Eagle Canoe Rentals (PO Box 4, Eagle City, AK, 99738, 907-547-2203, *paddleak@aptalaska.net*, *www.aptalaska.net/~paddleak*).

Lower Gulkana River

Another great road-accessible river float is the lower Gulkana River from Sourdough Campground on the Richardson Highway (mile 147.4) to the Richardson Highway Bridge (mile 127).

This is a good two-day float that covers 35 miles of class 1 and 2 water. This section of river is popular and is used by fishermen, boaters, and campers. It's a well-known river for catching king and silver salmon. Floating this river provides a good base for acquiring skills for longer excursions. Paddlers can stop the first night after 13 miles at the Poplar Grove Campground and then continue on the next day to the takeout.

For more information on floating the Gulkana River, consult the Gulkana River User Guide, available from the Bureau of Land Management (Glennallen Field Office, PO Box 147, Glennallen, AK 99588, 907-822-3217, *www.blm.gov/ak/gdo/index.html*).

THE ROAD TRIP TO END ALL ROAD TRIPS: DALTON HIGHWAY (HAUL ROAD)

Where: Starts 73 miles north of Fairbanks at the junction of the Elliot Highway, ends (for nonauthorized traffic) in Deadhorse
When: Open year-round
Length: 414 miles
Road condition: Rattle-your-teeth dirt and pavement
Services: Very scarce
Camping: Primitive campsites and pull-offs

Stay in this state very long, and you will soon travel all of our major highways, with the Dalton Highway reigning as king. Traveling this "highway" requires extra time, extra tires, and a willingness to throw yourself on the mercy of the high-speed truckers that own the road and hurl rocks at your windshield. You should not let this deter you from pulling on some adult diapers and trying it though.

Probably one of the most remote highways in the world, the 414-mile Dalton Highway is a high-speed dirt road to nowhere. Rental car companies prohibit vehicle use on this road and only the most cautious and prepared drivers are wise enough to travel it.

That said, the Dalton Highway offers travelers a truly amazing look at four cross-sections of wilderness in northern Alaska. From Fairbanks to Coldfoot, explorers will experience the boreal forest, dominated by permafrost soils and rolling hills, dotted with stunted black spruce. From Coldfoot, the landscape merges into the foothills of the Brooks Range until ascending 4,739-foot Atigun Pass to cross over the range and the Continental Divide. Rugged mountains with waterfalls and canyons infuse the landscape with awe-inspiring beauty. From Atigun Pass, travelers descend into the vast openness of the North Slope, with extreme stretches of treeless horizon. Farther north still comes the Arctic Coastal Plain and glimpses of migrating caribou, waterfowl, raptors, and shorebirds that inhabit this wind- and ice-shaped landscape.

There are virtually no services available, save for pricey gas, food, and basic amenities at the Yukon River Bridge (mile 56), Coldfoot (mile 175), and Deadhorse (mile 415). The road crosses over three mountain ranges—Brooks, Alaska, and Chugach—as well as thirty-four major and eight hundred minor rivers and streams.

The only regular traffic on this road is the long-haul truckers that run heavy loads on tight schedules back and forth to Prudhoe Bay. It is wise to pull over to the side of the road upon meeting them to let the dust dissipate and to reduce damage to your vehicle from flying gravel. You will want to have simple spare parts for your vehicle, extra gas, oil, and windshield wiper fluid, at least two full-size mounted spare tires, a tire jack, tools, and emergency flares. Drive with lights on at all times.

Weather can be unpredictable, considering that the journey traverses almost 500 miles starting at Fairbanks in the Interior and ending at the Arctic Ocean. Dressing in layers will allow you to adjust to the conditions, so don't skimp on warm clothing even if it is 80 degrees in Fairbanks. Prepare for bugs by bringing bug spray and head nets. You will definitely need both.

Although the road goes to the Arctic Ocean, you are only allowed to drive personal vehicles as far as Deadhorse. To go any further requires a purchased tour with a company that is authorized to do so. Stop at the hotel in Deadhorse for information, or call Tour Arctic/NANA (907-659-2368) or Prudhoe Bay Hotel Tours (907-659-2449).

For more information on traveling the Dalton Highway, contact the Bureau of Land Management (Fairbanks District Office, 1150 University Avenue, Fairbanks, AK 99709, 907-474-2200 or 800-437-7021, *www.blm.gov/ak/dalton/index.html*). Request (or download) the excellent publication called "Discover the Dalton," which covers everything you'll need to know about traveling this highway.

For road conditions, call the Alaska Department of Transportation's recorded information line by dialing 511. Also access their website for road conditions, advisories, roadwork updates, and more (*http://511.alaska.gov*).

ANOTHER GREAT ROAD TRIP: DENALI HIGHWAY

Where: Paxson to Cantwell
When: Summer only, closed in winter
Road condition: Dirt
Length: 135.5 miles
Services: Very scarce
Camping: Primitive campsites and pull-offs

The beautiful Denali Highway is a good way to burn a few days under the midnight sun. Definitely a road less traveled, the Denali Highway offers travelers a taste of untouched wilderness and jaw-dropping views of the Alaska Range while avoiding the hustle and bustle of other high-profile vacation destinations in the state. Before the Parks Highway was completed in 1972, the Denali Highway was the only road link to Denali National Park.

From Paxson to Cantwell, the highway extends 135.5 miles east and west and is open in the summer only. The condition of this rough road varies from good to "good grief!" Top speed is 40–45 miles per hour. The road has plenty of pull-offs and primitive campsites available for travelers, but services are scarce at best. It is best enjoyed over two or more days.

Popular with hunters, this road can become a busy place for a few short weeks in the fall. Hikers also enjoy the open expanses of the glacier-formed features in the area, and anglers will find excellent fishing in the lakes and streams accessible by foot or via off-road vehicles on selected trails.

The extra-adventurous traveler may opt to travel this road via mountain bike. As the traffic is sparse and usually slower, the Denali Highway makes for an excellent extended bicycle adventure.

For more information about traveling the Denali Highway, visit the highly informative Bureau of Land Management website (*www.blm.gov/ak/gdo/index.html*, click on "Denali Highway").

You may also want to consult *The Milepost*, a guide that offers mile-by-mile information for all major roads in Alaska (*www.themilepost.com*).

THE BACKPACKING TRIP TO END ALL BACKPACKING TRIPS: CHILKOOT TRAIL

If you're intent on going backpacking in Alaska, you'll want to buy a good hiking book. You might also want to look into hiring someone to carry your backpack for you, although some purists might pooh-pooh this.

My recommendation for one absolutely definitive Alaskan backpacking trip is the Chilkoot Trail, which follows the famous 1897 Klondike gold stampede route. After hearing about gold strikes on a tributary of the Klondike River in Yukon, Canada, gold seekers poured into Skagway from the Pacific coast to stake their claim on the supposed fortune. To get to the Klondike, they had to

How to End a Relationship: Take Your Partner Canoeing

There are many ways to break up with someone, but why not make your last moments together as memorable as possible? Canoeing sounds like a fun enough activity until you realize that one of you must steer and the other must navigate. This usually means that you will become aware of obstacles exactly two seconds before hitting them, when the navigator shouts out "Oh s[...]!"—at which point the person steering closes their eyes and growls just before the both of you hit the drink.

In other words, after four or five more scenarios just like the one above, you will hate each other. By the time the trip has ended, you will each be begging to end the relationship right then and there (a very tidy ending if you didn't want to be the bad guy).

This is also a good time to divide up your shared belongings. You will be so mad at each other that you will care less about who gets the Jackie Chan DVD collection and more about how fast you can set fire to the canoe. Although, if you had planned on keeping that new grill with the sweet built-in beverage cooler, I wouldn't bring it up now.

And that reminds me, drinking while canoeing will certainly tweak the situation just a bit. Someone will have to be reimbursed for the all lost beer, and that can get tricky.

It is always a good idea to bring friends along in another canoe to be witness to the final breakdown of the relationship. That way, when it comes down to the "he said, she said" banter that ultimately results, the only thing everyone will agree on is that "the next step" in your relationship should never have included a visit to the new Cabela's Superstore.

Canoe partners do not good lovers make.

Take heart though: the price of that boat was more than worth the hassle of a normal breakup. And you would never want to spend your life with someone who is an idiot on the water. On the other hand, you might have to live the rest of your life wondering who dunked whom.

hike over the Chilkoot Trail in order to reach the headwaters of the Yukon and then continue on to the goldfields—a total journey of over 600 miles.

This was no ordinary task though, as men were required to haul a year's worth of supplies over the steep, rugged pass. The Canadian North West Mounted Police Station stood at the top of the pass and checked every prospector for the proper supplies. No one was allowed to continue without the required gear. The 33-mile slog often took men months as they ferried gear back and forth from cache to cache, logging hundreds of miles in that short stretch alone. Historical artifacts can be easily observed from the trail, as all sorts of equipment and supplies were left behind.

Luckily, modern-day hikers don't have to cart a ton of supplies over the pass, but the terrain of the trail is the same as it was back then. Hikers are wise to research the trail description before embarking on this strenuous trip. For more information, contact the Klondike Gold Rush National Historic Park (*www.nps.gov/klgo*).

FUN THINGS TO DO THAT MIGHT KILL YOU

Climb Mount McKinley (Denali)

Attempting to climb Denali is a task undertaken by thousands of Alaska school children every year as a sort of final exam. As you can imagine, this is a tough test and many kids fail. This is how we keep our population in check (currently healthy at 600,000 plus) and ensure that we're not raising a bunch of sissies.

Alaska doesn't tolerate idiots, yet every year people from around the globe show up in Talkeetna for a shot at death as they attempt to climb Denali without the proper hall pass. We really like the view of Denali and prefer it not be littered with human carcasses. Be aware that just as Alaskans can supposedly control the northern lights with the flick of a switch, so it is with climbers on Denali. Start getting cocky, and we'll just vote you off the mountain.

If you're feeling lucky, go ahead and try to climb Denali. If we're in a good mood, we might just let you live.

Visit the Santa Claus House in North Pole

He looks innocent enough, the towering 100-foot giant Santa Claus that looms over the Richardson Highway standing adjacent to his Santa Claus RV Park and Christmas Ornament Empire. But really, have you taken a good look at Santa lately? He's ringed by a fence with barbed wire at the top (why?) and tethered to the ground by questionably skimpy wires. At any moment in a high wind Santa might break off and crush some hapless visitors, or come to life and take over Alaska, ruling over us with a spooky red-mittened fist. Take your chances. I for one recommend a perimeter of over 2,000 miles.

Replace Your Windshield

The enterprising genius who opened the first Windshield Repair and Replacement Center in Alaska was obviously thinking of the millions he would make by setting up shop here, in the Broken Windshield Capital of the World. What he didn't count on dealing with was the blood on his hands. Alaskans endure any number of flying objects hurled at their windshields on a daily basis, including suicidal moose that jump in front of our vehicles. Some drivers get notions of replacing their windshields only to be passed by a rock truck on the way home, in which case, there again goes the windshield. This scenario can only be repeated so many times before said windshield owner considers alternatives to windshield replacement. This usually includes a gun and a note. So don't replace that broken and chipped windshield. We're running out of burial plots.

AMAZING ALASKAN DESTINATIONS

I don't know how many times I've heard visitors say that their trip to Alaska was a "once in a lifetime" event for them. For those of us that live here, we wake up to the reality of our good fortune every day. The problem is how to see it all. Most of us will probably only see the smallest fraction of what Alaska has to offer in our lifetimes, but that doesn't mean we can't try. Here are my recommendations for some landmark places you should put at the top of your list.

Arctic National Wildlife Refuge

If there ever was a place worth defending, I think this is it. The debate over oil drilling has reached dizzying heights over the past couple years, and for now it looks like drilling may be narrowly averted. Encompassing 19.2 million acres, this is our nation's largest refuge and holds distinctive habitats for the many

How to Plaster-Cast Animal Tracks

Travel much in Alaska's backcountry and you will come across some impressive tracks left in mud or sand by our famed wildlife. I always travel with a medium-sized sealable plastic bag containing plaster of Paris so that I can make a cast if I find a really good print. I just add enough water directly to the bag to make the plaster into the consistency of pudding, or just a little runnier than that. Any water will do—from a stream, river, or lake, for instance.

Then I pour the plaster into the tracks and hang out while it hardens. This can take as little as five to ten minutes, depending on how thick or runny the mixture is and the weather conditions. Just after the cast has hardened up a bit, but before it's ready to extract from the track, I use a little stick to scribe the name of the animal that left the track and the location of the cast on the back of the plaster. You also might want to make an indentation the size of a nail at the top of the cast so that you can hang it up if you want. When dry, the cast should remove easily from the track.

I'd have to say that bear tracks are the hardest to cast because of the claws. That area doesn't take much plaster and breaks easily. Try to look for tracks around the edges of rivers, lakes, and other bodies of water. Plaster of Paris can be found in craft stores and hardware stores.

living creatures that call this place home. From the wide-open expanse of the Arctic Coastal Plain, to the mountainous peaks and arc of the Brooks Range, to the rolling landscape of the boreal forest to the south with its many lakes and rivers, this area is spectacular and vital.

Each year people come to this unfettered wilderness to witness the unending silence and walk where maybe no other human has before. They come to take a step back in time and discover a land that is the same as it has been for thousands of years.

For more information on traveling there, contact the U.S. Fish and Wildlife Service, Arctic National Wildlife Refuge (101 12th Avenue Room 236, Fairbanks AK 99701, 907-456-0250 or 800-362-4546, *arctic_refuge@fws.gov*, *http://arctic.fws.gov*).

McNeil River State Game Sanctuary

If it's bears you want to see, here's the place to find them. Located 200 miles southwest of Anchorage on the Alaska Peninsula, this site boasts the largest gathering of brown bears in the world at McNeil Falls. This is where the bruins come to feed on salmon that spawn from July through August. Over 140 bears have been reported here during a season, with over 72 bears counted at the falls on a single day.

Visitor access is limited to ten people per day, which has enabled a very successful record of bear/human coexistence and resource management. This destination is so popular that a lottery has been instituted to draw out the lucky visitors each season. Those fortunate enough to visit this area are closely attended by state biologists and given strict protocol to follow within the sanctuary. Visitors watch the bears from specified viewing platforms and camp and eat in designated areas. No bears have ever been killed in defense of life by visitors, and there have been no human injuries from bears since the program began. It is not uncommon for bears to pass within fifteen feet of visitors here. Nearby lands are scheduled to be opened up to bear hunting in late 2007, with much controversy, so see this special place while you can.

To enter the drawing for a permit, contact the Alaska Department of Fish and Game (907-267-2182, *www.wildlife.alaska.gov*, follow links to McNeil River State Game Sanctuary). You can also view live streaming video of the bears feeding at the falls on National Geographic's website (*www.ngm.com/wild camgrizzlies*) or through the Pratt Museum's website (*www.prattmuseum.org*).

Barrow

Seemingly at the top of the world, Barrow has the distinction of being the northernmost community in Alaska, as well as in North America. Located 330 miles north of the Arctic Circle, Barrow's 4,300 residents enjoy one of the harshest polar environments in Alaska. Despite this, there is beauty all around, and this Inupiat Eskimo community is steeped in tradition and history.

Modern conveniences and traditional living mesh in this northern town, but traditional culture plays out in everyday life. Eskimo men still hunt in the very celebrated fall and spring whale seasons, and the harvest is shared with the entire community.

The massive bird migrations that pass through Barrow are a big draw for visitors who yearn to see the fabled snowy owl that nests in the nearby tundra, as well as other "life list" birds.

The endless three months of sun in the summer and the reciprocal three months of darkness in the winter are a fact of life for residents and often a curious draw for visitors. Another draw to Barrow is the chance to have your picture taken in front of the welcome sign in town, which warns of roaming polar bears.

Comfortable accommodations can be easily found in Barrow, as can rental cars and tours for birding, photography, northern lights, and those that explore the cultural history of the region. There are no roads to Barrow, so the only way to reach the community is by air.

For more information about Barrow, visit the town's public radio station website (*www.kbrw.org*).

Valdez

If you want to visit the place where Alaskans go to play, Valdez is it. On any given day Valdez probably plays host to just as many Alaskans as out-of-staters. The latest craze for bumper stickers in Alaska now reads, "Valdez: Field-tested & Alaskan Approved," a message emblazoned on countless snowboards, bumpers, water bottles, and boat trailers across Alaska.

Surrounded by an incredible landscape of picture-perfect mountains joining the sea, Valdez makes a logical destination for anglers, boaters, sightseers, and campers. Come winter, with the average snowfall around 27 feet, Valdez becomes a playground for world-class heli-skiing and extreme snow machining. Ice climbing is also popular on the frozen waterfalls just off the Richardson Highway north of town.

What makes Valdez so charming, though, is its hometown feel. With only around four thousand residents, this community doesn't lose its roots come tourist season. In fact, the only tourist traffic the town sees these days comes down the highway in the form of RVs, and the town is especially popular with Fairbanksans who make the nearly 800-mile round-trip several times each summer. After years of declining stops, cruise ships completely abandoned Valdez as a port of call in 2005, citing Valdez's inability to accommodate the hordes of tourists that disembark the cruise ships and provide things for them to do.

That is not to say Valdez is lacking in activities for kayaking, sightseeing, rafting, fishing, or anything else that suits your fancy. In fact, Valdez has some of the best fishing I've ever experienced in my life. That there aren't any cruise ship crowds just means that it's easier to navigate the town and that there are less of those tacky T-shirt shops to avoid.

For more information about visiting Valdez, contact the Valdez Convention and Visitors Bureau (*www.valdezalaska.org*) or call the Valdez Visitors Information Center (800-770-5954).

THE BEST QUIRKY ATTRACTIONS IN ALASKA

I love Alaska for its independent spirit, and nothing epitomizes that spirit more than the following three off-beat attractions. Maybe you wouldn't go out of your way to see them, but if you happen to be driving by, they shouldn't be missed.

Mukluk Land

You can't miss the giant mukluk hanging under the sign at Mukluk Land in Tok, and you shouldn't miss a tour of this combination amusement park and museum. The kitschy collection has everything from dolls scavenged from the dump, to the building that housed Tok's first jail, to Santa's Rocket Ship (a must-see), to the cereal-box collection that will either make you smile or make you scratch your head. I love it. There's actually a lot of Alaska history here in the form of neglected items from various eras, and owners George and Beth Jacobs consider the stuff educational, yet admittedly hard to describe. As quoted in *Alaska & The Yukon*, George said, "That's been our biggest problem since we started, how do we describe it? It's a little bit of everything." Confirmed pack rats, George continued, "We're always trying to add more things to the park, provided that we think they're worthwhile." *Open June through August, mile 1317 Alaska Highway just outside of Tok, 907-883-2571.*

Wal-Mike's

Tongue in cheek, Wal-Mike's doesn't sell the kind of stuff you're used to at that other place. Instead you'll find an eclectic mix of antiques, consignment items, animal horns and hides, art, and—some might argue—junk. Be sure to ask about the human hand that sits in formaldehyde on the counter. Mike Carpenter is the entrepreneur behind the outfit, and he also plays dad to a couple reindeer that are tied out front for the amusement of visitors—although a sign posted nearby makes it clear that Mike is not responsible for their actions if you choose to get too friendly with them. *Mile 114 Parks Highway at Trapper Creek, 907-733-2637.*

Chicken

This tiny settlement of folks (around eleven total) on the Taylor Highway hosts the town with the famous name. Legend is that way back when, the locals wanted to call the new town Ptarmigan, after the state bird, but couldn't spell it. So they called it Chicken instead. Downtown Chicken is a funny thing. It is the only thing. A home-style restaurant, liquor store, mercantile, gift shop, gas station, and saloon make up most of it. You've got to go here and get a bumper sticker at the very least, and enjoy the ride on the beautiful, but mostly burned Taylor Highway. Of Chicken, Susan Wiren, owner of the saloon and most everything else, was quoted in *Alaska & The Yukon* as saying, "It's like a B-grade movie, that's all I'll say. You sit here for one week and you'll see everything you want to see or nothing, it's up to you." Look for information about Chicken in *The Milepost* (*www.themilepost.com*).

Quiz: Are You a Real Alaskan?

To separate those who know from those who should know better, here's a quiz to see where you rate on the scale of cheechako to sourdough. Don't worry though, the teacher has been drinking all night and your score will not affect her final hangover.

1. Bunny boots are:
a. rubber military-style boots good to 40 below
b. boots for children with cute bunny faces on the toes
c. what all the hippies are wearing in Girdwood
d. "girly" boots

2. Summer solstice takes place:
a. May 30
b. when mosquitoes begin mating
c. June 21
d. at first frost

3. An oosik is:
a. a fighting weapon used in the Alaska Fighting Championship
b. a stiff drink
c. the penis bone from a walrus
d. a mollusk

4. A "dry" cabin means:
a. the pipes froze
b. no alcohol is allowed
c. a cabin with a waterproof sod roof
d. there is no running water

5. Muskeg can be classified as:
a. an oversized party keg
b. bogs where little vegetation can grow
c. a scent gland from a Sitka black-tailed deer
d. skunky homebrew

6. You can catch hooligan:
a. with long handled dip nets
b. only if you don't wear a hat
c. from using a public shower
d. after two shots of tequila

7. The proper reaction to a charging bear is to:
a. call 911
b. shoot first, ask questions later
c. trip your friend
d. climb a tree

8. "Plugging in" refers to:
a. your Internet connection
b. prewarming your vehicle before starting it when it's cold
c. getting electricity
d. your hair replacement therapy

9. XTRATUFs are:
a. snow tires
b. Alaskan condoms
c. earmuffs for dogs
d. rubber boots

10. PFD stands for:
a. a brand of underwear
b. personal fishing device
c. permanent fund dividend
d. professional foot doctor

11. What is described as a "12-foot stare in a 10-foot room"?

a. cabin fever
b. a sighting of Bigfoot
c. TV addiction
d. a rabid fox

12. In 2000, Barb Everingham of Wasilla set a U.S. record at the state fair for what vegetable weighing over 105 pounds?

a. watermelon
b. zucchini
c. pumpkin
d. cabbage

13. "Breakup" means:

a. you better get out your XTRATUFs
b. you had an accident
c. the ice is breaking up on rivers
d. you quit dog mushing
e. both a and c

14. Nationwide, Alaskans rank number one and two respectively in their per capita consumption of:

a. alcohol and Nicorette gum
b. Yoo-hoo and Doritos
c. MREs and beef jerky
d. ice cream and Spam

15. A potlatch is:

a. the safety latch on a pressure cooker
b. a Native gathering to commemorate major life events
c. a place to hide marijuana
d. a pot holder

16. No-see-ums are:

a. tiny, silver-winged gnats
b. just a myth
c. hit-and-run drivers
d. blind moose

17. Robert Service is known for:

a. negotiating the purchase of Alaska from Russia
b. operating the first mail delivery system in Alaska (later known as UPS)
c. his colorful poetry about the gold rush days
d. his duet with Elvis Presley in Anchorage, 1968

18. If you live in the bush, you:

a. trap so you can afford TV
b. never cut your lawn
c. live off the road system
d. pay a lot for beer
e. all of the above

19. "Gee" and "haw" are commands used by:

a. ice fishermen
b. dog mushers
c. pilots
d. stock boys rounding up grocery carts

20. Hoarfrost is:

a. an Alaskan radio show
b. what happens when you spit in cold weather
c. frost that can build up to an inch or more in cold, windless regions
d. laryngitis brought on by the cold

21. If you've got a honey bucket, you:

a. keep honey bees

b. poop in a 5-gallon bucket

c. have a sweetheart

d. would rather keep this information private

e. both b and d

22. The number one necessity for an Alaskan vehicle is:

a. emergency flares

b. studded tires

c. a dog

d. expired plates

e. both c and d

23. If you are going Outside, it means:

a. you just need some fresh air

b. you're going to visit America (the Lower 48)

c. you have to go to the bathroom

d. the kids are driving you crazy

24. A fish wheel is:

a. a large current-driven wheel mounted in a river that catches fish

b. a contraption on your fishing rod that does all the work

c. what happens when you catch a halibut bigger than your boat

d. a term used when your boat trailer gets a flat

25. According to Alaskans, it's cold when:

a. you can no longer wear a T-shirt while dog mushing

b. you're going through three cords of wood a day instead of two

c. your bunny boots are in hiding

d. you're considering a vacation to northern Saskatchewan

e. all of the above

Scoring:

20-25 correct: Congratulations! You are now entered into a drawing for a log splitter!

16-19 correct: Not too bad, but fur underwear might have helped your score.

11-15 correct: You're not an idiot, but you're standing right next to him.

5-10 correct: Let me guess: The sun was in your eyes?

0-4 correct: I hear California is looking for more residents...

Answers: 1.a, 2.c, 3.c, 4.d, 5.b, 6.a, 7.b, 8.b, 9.d, 10.c, 11.a, 12.b, 13.e, 14.d, 15.b, 16.a, 17.c, 18.e, 19.b 20.c, 21.e, 22.e, 23.b, 24.a, 25.e

The Blue Tarp Challenge

This game is based on the premise that in almost every yard in Alaska you can find a blue tarp. The other things on this list are also common-place in the state. No matter where you go in Alaska, you'll probably find most of the things on this list. Play along and see what you can find. This game is best played on a road trip, while visiting Alaska on vacation, or with a bored group of friends on a Tuesday night.

Rules:

1 Divide into teams of two or more players.

2 Each team needs a pencil and a checklist. (Make copies of the checklist below to get you started.)

3 Create a set time to mark the checklist (e.g., the duration of a road trip).

4 Teams traveling by foot or bike get an automatic 15-point handicap.

5 At the end of the allotted time, all teams report back to an agreed upon meeting point.

6 Checklist points are tallied. The team with most points wins the distinction of being really quite observant and are treated to ice cream or beer by the losers. In case of a tie, arm-wrestle the other team, winner take all.

The Blue Tarp Challenge Checklist:

Item	Description	Point value	√ for each found
1	Find 5 yards in a row with blue tarps	5	☐
2	Find 10 yards in a row with blue tarps	10	☐
3	Find a BBQ grill on a porch	2	☐
4	Find 5 junked cars in 1 yard	10	☐
5	Spot a moose rack on a house	5	☐

6	Find a boat parked in someone's yard	2	☐
7	Spot an outhouse	5	☐
8	Spot a tourist	5	☐
9	Find a tourist trap	5	☐
10	Find someone wearing something that says "Alaska"	2	☐
11	Find a road sign with bullet holes	5	☐
12	Find a "No Shooting" sign with bullet holes	10	☐
13	Find frost heaves in a road	5	☐
14	Spot the Alaska Railroad	5	☐
15	Spot a dog in the back of a pickup	2	☐
16	Spot a Democratic bumper sticker	10	☐
17	Spot a hunting, mining, or NRA bumper sticker	5	☐
18	Find a cracked windshield	5	☐
19	Find a drive-thru espresso stand	5	☐
20	Spot an RV	2	☐
21	Spot a vehicle towing a boat	5	☐
22	Spot a Subaru	5	☐
23	Spot a vehicle with a dog box	10	☐
24	Spot a man with long hair	5	☐
25	Find someone with a backpack	5	☐
26	Spot someone fishing	5	☐
27	Find someone riding an ATV	5	☐
28	Find someone tent camping	5	☐
29	Find someone wearing XTRATUFs (fisherman-style rubber boots)	5	☐
30	Find someone wearing bunny boots (winter rubber boots)	10	☐
31	Find someone playing a musical instrument	10	☐
32	Find someone wearing Carhartts	5	☐
33	Find someone wearing fur	10	☐
34	Find someone with a Leatherman on their belt	5	☐
35	Spot the Alaska State Ferry	5	☐
36	Spot a commercial fishing boat	5	☐
37	Find someone kayaking, rafting, or canoeing	10	☐
38	Spot a seagull	2	☐
39	Spot someone cleaning fish	5	☐
40	Spot a cruise ship	2	☐

41	Spot a whale	20	☐
42	Spot a sea otter or sea lion	10	☐
43	Find a totem pole	5	☐
44	Spot a float plane	5	☐
45	Spot a glacier	5	☐
46	Spot a moose	10	☐
47	Spot Mount McKinley (Denali)	5	☐
48	Spot a bear or a wolf	20	☐
49	Spot an eagle	10	☐
50	Find Alaska beer on a menu	2	☐
51	Spot the Alaska state bird (ptarmigan)	10	☐
52	Spot the Alaska state flag	5	☐
53	Spot a dog yard (a place where mushers keep their many dogs)	5	☐
54	Find a mounted bear	5	☐
55	Find a mounted fish	5	☐
56	Spot the northern lights	10	☐
57	Spot a log cabin	5	☐
58	Find some fireweed	2	☐
59	Find a giant vegetable in a garden or at the fair	5	☐
60	Spot a raven	5	☐
61	Find some wild berries	5	☐
62	Find snow in May	10	☐
63	Find some devil's club	5	☐
64	Find a wild animal track	5	☐

Grand Total:

Index

About the Author

Brookelyn Bellinger grew up in rural Michigan and had dreams of moving to Alaska by the time she reached high school. She cemented this notion after her first trip to the state at age 19. It wasn't long after she was declaring herself a resident and was anxiously awaiting October and the issuance of the oil check.

To support her outdoor habits, Brookelyn obtained a bachelor's degree in outdoor/adventure recreation management and then successfully applied her education to jobs such as waiting tables, baking for a coffee house, and working in a chocolate shop. In between, she worked as an outdoor educator, recreation director, guide, wildland firefighter, and ski bum. She also released a CD of pop/folk originals as a singer-songwriter.

Brookelyn's writing has appeared in major magazines, and she was most recently enjoying notoriety as a Fairbanks humor columnist before she got canned. More information can be gleaned from her website, *www.brookelyn bellinger.com*, as well as prompts to buy her book, her CD, and other stuff. Brookelyn currently lives with her family in Delta Junction, Alaska, and works for the tiny local newspaper.